XTREME HOUSES

COURTENAY SMITH + SEAN TOPHAM

PRESTEL

MUNICH · BERLIN · LONDON · NEW YORK

PRESTEL VERLAG, MUNICH · BERLIN · LONDON · NEW YORK, 2002

© FOR CONCEPT AND TEXT BY COURTENAY SMITH AND SEAN TOPHAM, 2002

THE RIGHT OF COURTENAY SMITH AND SEAN TOPHAM TO BE IDENTIFIED AS AUTHORS OF THIS WORK
HAS BEEN ASSERTED IN ACCORDANCE WITH THE COPYRIGHT, DESIGN, AND PATENTS ACT 1988.

COVER: DOUG JACKSON, *CASA VERTICAL*, 2000
FRONTISPIECE: SOFTROOM, *TREE HOUSE*, 1998
PHOTO CREDITS: SEE PAGE 167

PRESTEL BOOKS ARE AVAILABLE WORLDWIDE.
VISIT OUR WEB SITE AT WWW.PRESTEL.COM OR CONTACT ONE OF THE FOLLOWING PRESTEL OFFICES FOR FURTHER INFORMATION.

PRESTEL VERLAG
KÖNIGINSTRASSE 9, 80539 MUNICH
TEL. +49 (89) 38 17 09-0, FAX +49 (89) 38 17 09-35
E-MAIL: SALES@PRESTEL.DE

PRESTEL PUBLISHING
4 BLOOMSBURY PLACE, LONDON WC1A 2QA
TEL. +44 (20) 7323-5004, FAX +44 (20) 7636-8004
E-MAIL: SALES@PRESTEL-UK.CO.UK

PRESTEL PUBLISHING
175 FIFTH AVENUE, NEW YORK 10010
TEL. +1 (212) 995-2720, FAX +1 (212) 995-2733
E-MAIL: SALES@PRESTEL-USA.COM

LIBRARY OF CONGRESS CONTROL NUMBER: 2002112194
DIE DEUTSCHE BIBLIOTHEK LISTS THIS PUBLICATION IN THE DEUTSCHE NATIONALBIBLIOGRAFIE;
DETAILED BIBLIOGRAPHIC DATA IS AVAILABLE ON THE INTERNET AT HTTP://DNB.DDB.DE

DESIGN AND TYPOGRAPHY BY SMITH, LONDON
PRINTED AND BOUND BY PASSAVIA DRUCKSERVICE, PASSAU

PRINTED IN GERMANY ON ACID-FREE PAPER

ISBN 3-7913-2789-5

WE ARE ALL ARCHITECTS

we are not architects. Nor have we ever studied architecture proper. we have, however, spent pretty much all of our lives living in some sort of house and have shaped those houses to better suit our needs, which we guess makes us architects along with everyone else who has made a decision about the place they call home.

we are curious about what exactly constitutes a house, or in fact a home, since a "house" is all about an individual approach to shelter and "housing" is about dwelling on a mass scale. To us, housing is a blanket solution that treats everyone the same. It is homogeneous and often boring. However, houses are unique and allow for one person's perception of "home" to be completely different from another's. Sensing that there had to be more than one perfect "house," we started to look at the rush of activity in domestic design. What we discovered might be described as the leading edge of residential architecture, although it's certainly not advertised—at least not yet—at real estate offices or in the property pages.

The homes presented herein are extreme in the sense that they are exceptional, radical, and on the edge. Certain examples may not look excessive but that is because we have concerned ourselves with content rather than style. Each house has been chosen because it poses a challenge to traditional methods or attempts to solve a problem. There are plenty of homes out there that may look extreme, but for the most part these are mere follies which enrich the fabric of their local communities as curiosities. All too often they fail to make a social impact when placed in a broader context.

Our choice of houses has been determined by their relevance to today's global community. The selection of homes that follows in this book represents an exchange of ideas from the far ends of the international social spectrum. Many would have passed away unheard of if it weren't for the Internet's capability to communicate information from the ends of the earth. The global communications network established by the First World has brought its innovations—for better or worse—to bear on lifestyle, including housing, in the Third World, and vice versa. In fact the Third World has demonstrated time and again that necessity is the mother of invention when it comes to home design. In countries of limited resources, individuals, architects, and builders must look beyond materials and methods typically associated with house construction, an approach that is beginning to broaden the mindset of architects in the west. Westerners would do well to start lending as much credence and attention to, say, the temporary shelters that accommodate our construction workers, as to the buildings the workers erect.

In certain cases, the houses we have chosen literally occupy the fringes of society, while in other cases they are completely remote from it and located in extreme environ-ments or extreme social situations. They also respond to extraordinary conditions, including unprecedented mobility, natural disasters, war, population shifts, and homelessness. The homes selected almost always introduce new or forgotten technologies and materials appropriated from sources as diverse as Middle Eastern engineering to the film, automotive, aerospace, and fashion industries, resulting in forms that engender new ways of interacting with each other and our environment.

An issue that is thoroughly investigated is homelessness, which takes on different guises depending on context. In western cities, it is often the result of misfortune, negligence, or choice, while in unsettled or unindustrialized nations it is the result of abject poverty, civil war, discrimination, or governmental oppression.

Also looked at in detail is the impact of glob-alization and consumer culture on the housing industry. In some instances, it is westerners who are leading the way in affordable housing for Third World countries—whether through the use of domes made of sandbags or the manufacture of portable shelters—but their designs are not always welcomed by those who need them most, people who want nothing more than to live in western-style bungalows with televisions. At the same time,

globalization has also opened the door for immigration and the world is an increasingly mixed ethnic bag for it. This was always true in urban centers, the landing place of foreign workers throughout the nineteenth and twen-tieth centuries. But now smaller cities are exploding with cultural difference and desire. In the United States, this is nowhere more obvious than the suburbs, where ethnic home-owners are steadily replacing, or displacing, the "white bread" settlers of fifty years hence.

Never before have we been such a mobile society, able to communicate with friends and family from any imaginable location or to hop on a flight across the world at the drop of a hat. This migratory impulse, coupled with a shift in tourism away from luxury spas and resorts to packaged vacations in "authentic" locales—whether a Masai-owned lodge in Kenya or a Russian gulag—has increased westerners' understanding of how the other half lives and opened a pipeline for the exchange of cultural ideas.

Admittedly there is a preponderance of "extreme" creativity to draw upon at the moment, whether from architects, artists, collectives, or individuals. What we present herein is a short list of what's out there, a sampling that is by no means finite or exclusive

we Are All Architects, courtenay smith and sean Topham

but representative of a broad spectrum of builders and building types from a number of continents, including Africa, Australia, Asia, Europe, and North America. Likewise, we have grouped our picks into loose and open-ended categories that reflect many of the ideas and techniques being tossed about these days. The intention was to allow concepts from one category to spill over to another without nailing them down to any single, hermetically sealed "movement" or "style."

The chapter entitled "self-construct" covers a wide range of self-build strategies in an equally wide range of contexts. In First world countries, designing and building a home yourself is a luxury, while in the Third world it is simply a necessity. What passes for experimentation in one context, passes for protection in another—even though both examples may be informed by similar techniques. Self-building in both contexts is almost always liberating, although the oppressors are usually radically different. In one world it's poverty, in another it's not getting enough quality housing for your money.

"Move to the sticks" is about ditching the rigors of the city altogether and moving out into the country. It encompasses the extremes of poverty and luxury as is evident in the sharp divide between the basic shelter and the lavish retreat. However, we steer clear of the traditional country house and instead portray the rural environment as an exciting testing ground for new ideas and innovations that challenge the monotonous tedium of urban housing schemes and question the relationship of nature to culture.

"Bring your own building" looks at nomadic living systems and how architects are coping with the impact of increased mobility. There is a great blurring of boundaries in this chapter with vehicles, portable pods, and even articles of clothing vying to be justly recognized as architecture. The American collective Ant Farm, Austrian-based Haus-Rucker-Co, and English architects Archigram are huge influences here. Seminal nomadic projects such as Archigram's *suitaloon* (1968) and *cushicle* (1966) were launched in an era when society was not quite ready for any traveling building other than a caravan. Nowadays, with global communications technology and affordable travel, people seem to be switching on to the notion of the take-anywhere home.

"Fitting in," both socially and physically, is the primary theme of the homes in the final chapter, "space invaders." As inhabitants of large hubs already know, the price of living in an exciting city is usually having less personal space in which to maneuver or live. With real estate prices skyrocketing in urban centers around the globe, the need for adequate housing at affordable prices is pressing, and architects, artists, and individuals are responding with wit and imagination rather than despair. Some of their solutions even border on the guerrilla but then the market itself has never been particularly democratic. People are often forced to make do with shoddy one-room studios, leaking, turn-of-the-century fire hazards, or brutal mid-rises that drain the spirit. It is no wonder that people have responded by laying claim to as much space as they can with homes that latch onto public buildings, additions that hang out of windows, or shelters which suck energy from existing power sources.

The domestic architecture scene is alive with new ideas and designs for living, and these small-scale projects are providing the ideal vehicle for a new generation of architects as well as practitioners from other disciplines to make a statement about how we live. Rather than merely complaining, individuals from all walks of life are taking direct action by reaching for their tools and designing their own homes, as evidenced by the explosion of home improvement television shows, evening classes in *feng shui*, and huge DIY stores. And to architects, the house has become what the seven-inch single was to punk bands. It is a liberating challenge for its designer and an immediate, accessible product for the end user.

The renewed interest in individual houses is a refreshing development for contemporary architecture. In a recent feature in *Architectural Review*, editor Peter Davey wrote, "thirty or forty years ago it was considered vulgar in architectural circles to talk about 'homes': that was left to the commercial providers of tacky repro semi-detached villas."[1] If the projects in this book are anything to go by, the architects of today are learning a valuable lesson from those commercial manufacturers in giving people what they want. This is why you will also find a selection of industrial shelters, lifestyle accessories, and self-build kits from outside the usual realm of architecture included in this book.

At the same time, it is important to point out that there was a time in recent history when architects were talking a great deal about what a "home" should be. And in the opinion of "great white gods,"[2] such as Walter Gropius or Mies van der Rohe, it wasn't the aristocratic country estates or bourgeois Victorian brown-

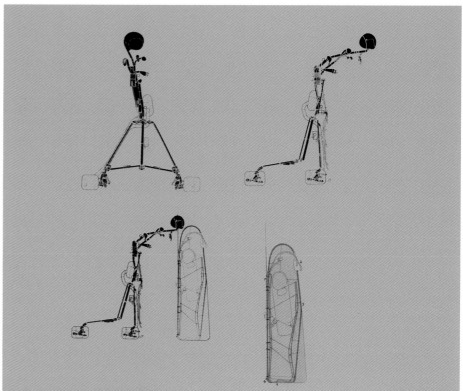

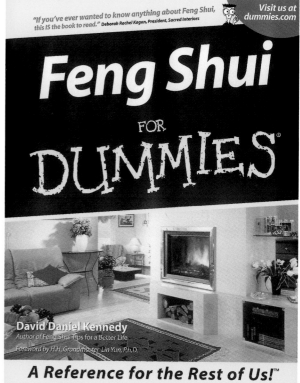

Feng Shui
FOR
DUMMIES

David Daniel Kennedy
Author of Feng Shui Tips for a Better Life
Foreword by H.H. Grandmaster Lin Yun, Ph.D.

A Reference for the Rest of Us!™

stones of pre-WWI Europe. For perhaps the first time in history, the ordinary house became a focus of architectural theory and practice. As little as seventy years ago, the Modernist credo of pure form and "starting from zero"[3]—which we typically associate with severe, undecorated corporate high rises, art galleries, or school campuses—had already taken root in radical residential commissions, from Gerrit Rietveld's *Schroeder House* (1924) in Utrecht, The Netherlands, to Le Corbusier's *Villa Savoye* (1931) in Poissy, France, to Mies van der Rohe's *Farnsworth House* (1949) in Plano, Illinois. This minimal abstract style was transported into worker housing in Europe and eventually recycled as luxury apartments in the United States. Endemic to all cases was that a theoretical imperative had found its expression in the fundamental unit of any society—the home—signaling that huge intellectual shifts could just as easily take place on a small scale. When exploring the homes in this book, it is important to keep in mind that their "extreme" ideas may already be well on their way to defining our greater cultural and social landscape.

Pop culture's obsession with all things retro over the last decade has delivered a blurry-eyed nostalgia for the commercially manufactured dwellings and mobile homes of the 1950s and beyond, but nobody is shedding tears over the architect-designed high-rise and high-density housing schemes of that same era. In the postwar reconstruction of Europe, architects and urban planners imposed their grand schemes onto a society that was never properly consulted about how it wanted to live. The common solution to housing across Europe was to build a box, place a family in it, and demand that they shape their life around it. Is it any wonder then that some inhabitants of these estates decided to use the elevators as toilets? Dissatisfaction with the dysfunctional machines for living was voiced loudly throughout the following decades, from grassroots organizations to rock bands, and is most poignantly summed up in the lyrics of The Jam: "They were going to build communities. It was going to be pie in the sky. But the piss-stenched hallways and broken down lifts said the planner's dream went wrong." Thankfully the architect's role in the provision of homes appears to have switched from that of dictator to more of a facilitator. Architects are becoming tailors and the house a bespoke suit for living in. Major contributing factors to this shift are the recent advances in construction technology and the unprecedented role of the individual in the design process.

Computer-aided design and computer numerically controlled production are making our homes more expressive if not more sculptural, and technical advances in industries as far afield as the movies and aerospace are finding their way into the toolboxes of today's residential architects. Architect Doug Garofalo has found that working with Maya, an animation software, has enabled him to design house additions with radically free-flowing curves never before possible with a jigsaw. Likewise, Greg Lynn FORM is able to tailor-make homes on a mass scale by working with computers that communicate directly with the machines that give physical form to the studio's designs. Mass production and prefabrication no longer mean bland uniformity, nor are professional architects the sole beneficiaries of the new technologies. With computers being as integral to every household as a telephone, potential homeowners can now customize, order, and, in some cases, even download plans for their dream homes via the Internet. Sites such as Etekt.com offer everyday folks the chance to "co-create" their home by browsing a variety of architectural firms and customizable homes for purchase.[4] After selecting a model from a library of home designs, buyers may use parametric design software to add on rooms or change materials before settling on a final plan which an architect then issues—the entire process mediated by the web.

For probably the first time in recent architectural history, the individual is playing a leading rather than supporting role in how houses come into being. To be sure, in the years following WW2, private individuals across Europe and America assumed a variety of functions, from client to end user to self-builder, but in all cases at the subordination of either a visionary architect or developer. Throughout the 1950s and 1960s private clients bankrolled the severe white cubes imposed on them by architects who "knew better" and watched as their everyday needs and possessions receded, quite literally, into the background. The disputes between Edith Farnsworth and Mies van der Rohe over her need for private areas in his otherwise exposed "art gallery" design are legendary. But what she got out of the deal were two hidden bathrooms which didn't interrupt his plan. And this, at a time when an explosion of literature on home styling and a profusion of furnishings and accessories (from dinnerware to wallpaper) were enabling Americans to search for their identities through products.

We Are All Architects, Courtenay Smith and Sean Topham

TOP LEFT IT IS INCREASINGLY EASY FOR HOMEBUYERS TO DESIGN THEIR HOUSES USING THE INTERNET. ETEKT.COM IS AN ON-LINE ARCHITECTURAL STUDIO THAT ALLOWS PRIVATE CLIENTS TO ACCESS AFFORDABLE, ARCHITECTURAL PLANNING DOCUMENTS FOR NEW RESIDENCES. THE SITE'S CUSTOMIZEABLE MODELS ARE FUNKY ALTERNATIVES TO THE CAPE COD OR RANCH HOUSES MANY OF US STILL THINK OF AS HOME.

TOP RIGHT ARCHITECTURAL RENDERING OF ONE OF THE MODELS OF THE CAPE COD HOUSE BUILT IN LEVITTOWN, LONG ISLAND, 1947. THIS VERNACULAR STYLE CONTINUES TO PREDOMINATE AS A WESTERN SYMBOL OF "HOME."

BOTTOM UNFORTUNATELY, THE CAPE COD WASN'T SUITED TO A VARIETY OF LIFESTYLE NEEDS AND THEREFORE HAD TO BE PERIODICALLY UPDATED WITH EXTENSIONS SUCH AS THESE.

on the suburban front, things weren't much better. Developers liked to maintain the illusion that end users were really clients being provided the service of affordable, attractive housing. But the reality was that the client was merely the "user" of what the developer provided. Although prefabrication allowed various elements of the homes to be produced off site, it also left little room for changes outside manufacturer-defined limits. The typical tract home consisted of four rooms, regardless of how large or diverse a family might be. In many cases, home improvement was needed before the house even hit the ground, a developer-programmed "detail," which cost the user more money in the end and laid the foundation for the DIY phenomenon.

Today, homeowners have fewer knee-jerk reactions where architects and developers are concerned. In today's global service economy, the terms "client," "end user," and "self-builder" have taken on new meanings connoting control and leadership not subservience. The buying power of the consumer, good or bad, can no longer be ignored, and for a "provider" to do so would be to limit his or her client base to bankruptcy. The term client now implies that people will pay only for what they commission. An end user will bring the product back to the

source if it doesn't work or suit his needs. And those who self-build are akin to the new visionaries, striking out on their own, both aesthetically and technically.

The single prevailing belief expressed by most of the architects in this book is in a collaborative approach to the design of the home. The architects we consulted have affirmed time and again that cooperation between designer and end user is essential to producing a successful building. This collaborative approach appears in as many different guises as the homes themselves. It can take the form of workshops with homeless individuals, as practiced by Studio Orta and Krzysztof Wodiczko, how-to seminars such as those offered by the Monolithic Dome Institute or Earthship Biotecture, hands-on, three-dimensional tools to communicate ideas, as developed by Coelacanth & Associates, or a studio dynamic structured around the collision of ideas, as in the collectives FAT, PO.D, N55, openoffice, and Atelier van Lieshout. The architects seem in agreement that they arrive at the best possible solution by working with the end user and involving that person in the decision-making process.

Flexibility is another key factor the houses here have in common. In the nineteenth

century, a house was made up of rooms, each with a preordained purpose. Although many people still live in homes built during that era, the permanence of the structure in these dwellings renders them difficult to adaptation and change. The people behind the homes in this book have adopted the belief that the only thing we can be sure of is change and incorporate future-proofing elements into their designs. For some, this means eliminating rooms altogether to make way for an open, flexible space with which the inhabitant does as he or she pleases, as can be seen in Shigeru Ban's *Naked House* and Doug Jackson's *casa vertical*. Others, like Alles wird Gut and Office of Mobile Design, have adopted the foldaway ingenuity of the Swiss Army knife and brought the utility of the multifunction tool into the home. Then there are homes with a finite life span, such as those by Lacaton & Vassal. These are not throwaway in the same sense as was popular in the 1960s, but they are responsible to the environment and have a low impact when it comes to disposing of them.

Buying a house is one of the biggest expenses we ever incur, but need it be? One area where costs can be reduced and is undergoing great experimentation is the domestic application of building materials usually

reserved for industry. Fewer of us work in the manufacturing industry than ever before and the industrial era is now in visible decline. Heavy industrial machinery that once seemed threatening and even dehumanizing is now looked upon with nostalgia. The extensive search for new spaces to inhabit is partly illustrated by the number of architects who are making homes from disused freight containers and shunting industrial construction technology into the home. If the work of LOT/EK, Doug Jackson, and Jones, Partners: Architecture is anything to go by, then homeowners today are willing to live amongst great slices of heavy industry. Loft apartments in the disused factories of New York were an early indication that dead industrial space could be remolded into a domestic dwelling. Their success is a perfect example of how attitudes to living space can change drastically.

In contrast to this, other projects revive materials that have largely been forgotten since the onset of the industrial revolution. Hay bales, as used in Sarah Wigglesworth's *9 stock orchard street*, are cheap and simple to build with and also have excellent insulation properties. Other architects have taken such traditional techniques and updated them with new materials. Rural Studio and Shigeru Ban, like

WE ARE ALL ARCHITECTS, COURTENAY SMITH AND SEAN TOPHAM

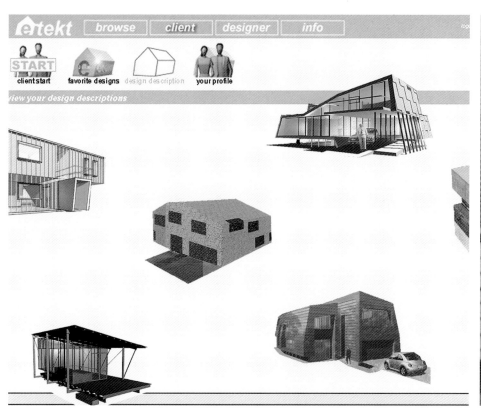

(a)

(b)

(c)

1 Peter Davey, "Architecture, Dwelling and the Global Market," *The Architectural Review*, volume CCXX, no. 1253, London, July 2001.

2 Tom Wolfe, *From Bauhaus to Our House*, (New York: Farrar Straus Giroux, 1981), 46.

3 Ibid, 14.

4 Eric Howeler, "soft serve," *Praxis*, vol. 3, 2002, 98.

5 Mike Davis, *City of Quartz*, (New York: Vintage, 1990).

6 Criminal Justice and Public Order Act 1994, Part 5, sections 61, 77, and 80, Her Majesty's stationery office: www.hmso.gov.uk

the pioneers of early vernacular architecture, are investigating abundant materials like paper, which would otherwise be considered as waste, and expanding the scope of construction technology with remarkable results. Moreover, collectives such as Cal-Earth or Earthship Biotecture are turning to the earth itself and using soil as a sustainable, readily available building material.

The majority of us spend most of our lives working in order to pay for a home. The lack of choice in the mainstream housing market means that often we have to compromise with a poor design in order to put a roof over our heads. With so much money and effort channeled into the purchase of a home, one has to ask why it is that so many of us do not obtain exactly what we want. When we buy a car we don't buy a green model when we want it in red, but when we buy a home we are prepared to overlook such matters as the bathroom being too small or a window being in the wrong place. Many of the projects we have included are generated out of sheer frustration at the lack of quality, affordable houses where the emphasis is on usability rather than maximum profits for a property developer.

This distinct lack of choice is a major restriction on our personal freedom.

collectives such as N55 and Atelier van Lieshout are eager to point out that it is the state authorities and commercial developers who govern the way we live. They urge us to question the amount of freedom we, as citizens of western democracies, actually have when it comes to choosing how we live. When it comes to acquiring a home, our freedom of choice is questionable. All too often freedom is taken from those who have chosen to take control over the most important decisions affecting their immediate environment. Life is made very difficult for the person who breaks the mold. Freedom-loving Americans are quick to forget their pioneering, nomadic past when enacting city ordinances against beggars and the homeless—often in the language and style of war. As author Mike Davis pointed out in his 1990 book, *City of Quartz*, city councils have spared no cost on barrel-shaped benches, sprinkler systems, and pronged trash cages that prohibit any unsuspecting wanderer from living in an alternative way on public property.[5] As recently as last year, New York City still had anti-homeless laws in place that forbid illegal camping, that is, the construction or use of any structure more than three and a half feet high—the size of a tent—on the city's streets or in its parks.

By opting out of mainstream society you become an outsider, a freak even. Nomadic communities in particular, by the nature of their way of life, are forced to live at the very edge of the regulations laid down to govern a nation's citizens. The nomadic existence has long been scorned upon. In European history, the static societies of the ancient Greeks and Romans are generally considered to be the "great" civilizations, whereas the nomadic tribes, loosely labeled as the Barbarians, are wrongly thought of as primitive savages, largely due to there being no towering stone monuments to their existence. In England, the 1994 Criminal Justice and Public Order Act effectively outlawed the nomadic way of life.[6] The Act was introduced to put a stop to all night rave parties and encampments of New Age travelers, but its impact on gypsies and anyone else wishing to adopt a nomadic lifestyle is devastating.

Neither of us are specialists and we are unlikely to impart any droplets of divine wisdom. If anything we ask questions rather than offer solutions. We have taken the liberty to speak about how homes are, or could be, designed, from the point of view of two people who are "housed." Although both of us are from western, postindustrial democracies, we

have completely different backgrounds and viewpoints. Courtenay Smith's point of view is unapologetically informed by the highway culture and edge city sprawl of Dallas, Texas, with a final cross over into old-world density via Munich, Germany. Sean Topham's outlook has been formed by his life in the industrial north of England and now London, a ridiculously expensive city as far as the housing market is concerned. Together we draw on our experiences as travelers, being ourselves products of the increasingly mobile global economy.

In a way this book has been a revelation of our subconscious belief, or resignation, that we would never own a home. We came to this conclusion independently and then together but always for the same reasons. First, we are simply too poor to own property. Second, and probably because we are poor, we demand more bang for our buck and are not willing to compromise on quality.

Prior to researching this book, the idea of living out our days in rented apartments in lively urban centers seemed more than just a practical solution, but a given. Now each of us is considering a little home improvement of our own. A dome in the country? An inflatable shelter in the city? A freight container in the suburbs? The possibilities are rife.

We Are All Architects, Courtenay Smith and Sean Topham

THERE'S NO PLACE LIKE HOME

CHAPTER 1

SELF-CONSTRUCT

HOUSES in the city cost too much and they're often poorly made. Rather than compromise with a suspect property developer or leave it up to a shoddy builder, why not construct your own home—in the shape you want and the location you desire?

Running the gamut from the idiosyncratic and expressionistic to the commercially abetted, the homes in this chapter demonstrate the wide range of currently available and evolving self-build strategies in an equally wide range of contexts. There is still a frontier spirit of wanting to strike out on one's own, and in all of these scenarios the parties involved are dissatisfied with quickly obsolete prefabs, boring floor plans, or the lack of affordable housing period. More and more homeowners desire custom-made dwellings that suit eclectic tastes and needs.

On one end of the spectrum are individuals who, for varying reasons, are taking the matter of housing into their own hands. In certain instances, the need for self-expression in a market dominated by look-a-like homes with thirty-year mortgages assumes precedence over practical considerations or traditional materials, as in sculptor Robert Bruno's *Steel House* and Jessica Stockholder's proposal for *Houses x Artists*. In other cases, the desire to inhabit a home that is crossbred with another function provides the impetus for experimentation, as in artist Vito Acconci's *House of Cars #2*.

Related to this are the efforts of architects to bring housing back into a more collaborative, open-ended dialogue with homeowners. Often this means working closely with individuals who lack technical know-how but desire a unique solution to their living situation. This can take the form of fantasy additions such as Koeppel & Martinez's *schlafhaus* or radical extensions to existing homes as in Doug Garofalo's *Markow* and *Manilow* residences. The synergistic nature of these commissions paves the way for better communication and exchange between client/builder and architect/provider and often results in new-fangled shapes, proportions, and angles.

Architects themselves are also going it alone in order to arrive at the kind of dwellings they themselves would like to inhabit. London-based Sarah Wigglesworth risked financial and physical bankruptcy to try out the viability of sandbags and hay bales as alternative building materials for her home/office at *9 Stock Orchard Street* in London. Likewise, the UK collective FAT do not compromise when it comes to envisioning their ideal quarters. Their homes are fantasy driven and indulge taste over space.

At the other end of the spectrum are self-builders in poorer countries for whom DIY is not a luxury but a necessity. Across the board, these individuals require immediate shelter and seek out building materials that are readily available, durable, and cheap. In Lesotho, South Africa, German engineer Michael Hoenes incorporates tin cans as the primary building block of his one-room houses. While in Jamaica, Richard J. L. Martin, along with the not-for-profit *Global Peace Containers* organization, is turning First World industrial leftovers—freight containers—into quick and safe homes for locals. Typically, the people who need shelter the most don't have the time to wait for their homes to be built and therefore physically contribute to their construction. This is nowhere more evident than in Amman, Jordan, where residents of East Wahdat work together to upgrade each other's shanties.

Between these two extremes are companies that provide the tools and supplies for the layman in any context to house himself. Florida-based American Ingenuity holds classes and publishes instructions on how to build geodesic domes, while the Monolithic Dome Institute in Texas has patented an inflatable balloon that enables any self-builder to design and construct his own concrete shell. Both types of home are flexible, transportable, and strong enough to function in environments ranging from beach fronts to fault lines. This is also true of the *Briggs Port-A-Fold shelter system*, whose incredibly sturdy modules can be conjoined endlessly and, with a little imagination, transformed into tailor-made homes in war-torn nations or peaceful backwaters.

Starting from zero no longer means departing from someone else's point of reference, although it does have different connotations depending on one's context. In some cultures, beginning at the beginning can result in the perfect house in the perfect location. In others, starting from scratch yields homes that many would never have dreamed of owning.

FAT

House in Hackney, London, England 2002
Anti Oedipal House, prototype dwelling, 2000
Semi-Dysfunctional House, prototype dwelling, 2000

BELOW FAT HAVE SAMPLED AND REMIXED DETAILS FROM OTHER ARCHITECTURAL STYLES. THE BEDROOM RESIDES BEHIND OFFICE BLOCK WINDOWS, AND THE HOUSE IS TOPPED WITH ORNAMENTAL MOTIFS TAKEN FROM CANAL-SIDE BUILDINGS IN AMSTERDAM.

RIGHT *HOUSE IN HACKNEY.* THE WOODEN CLADDING GIVES THE IMPRESSION OF A THEATRICAL CONSTRUCTION SUCH AS A TEMPORARY MOVIE SET OR WOBBLY, ON-STAGE SCENERY.

FAT (Fashion Architecture Taste), London, England

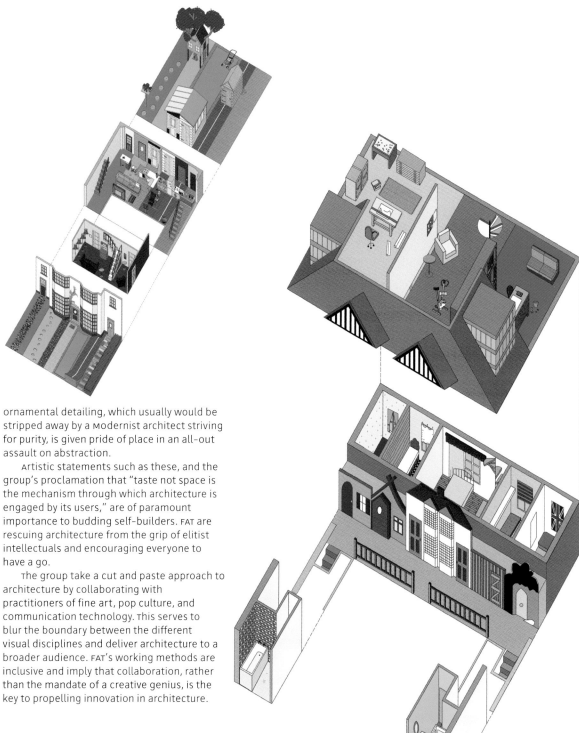

FAT urges us all to kill the Modernist within. *Anti Oedipal House* is armed with an acidic wit that targets the Modernist tenet that form should follow function. *Anti Oedipal House* is the result of form following dysfunction and is designed to accommodate a married couple and their teenage son, while also satisfying each individual's respective fantasy. The parents are able to fulfill their shallow lifestyle aspirations by holding dinner parties in their pristine glass house. Meanwhile, the son is free to indulge in his adolescent obsessions away from his parents' repressive gaze in the voluptuous, pink "mastabatorium." In a similar proposal, *semi-dysfunctional House*, two suburban, semidetached houses are remodeled to give each family member his or her own strip of private living space. The family has to come together only in the reception area when a display of unity is required to please visiting friends or relatives.

FAT (Fashion Architecture Taste) believes the house is not just a machine for living in but a home brimming with sentiment and a sense of place. The inhabitant makes it his own by decorating it to reflect his personal taste. In the built project *House in Hackney*, the architects take a swipe at the Modernist sensibility of "less is more." Here the ornamental detailing, which usually would be stripped away by a Modernist architect striving for purity, is given pride of place in an all-out assault on abstraction.

Artistic statements such as these, and the group's proclamation that "taste not space is the mechanism through which architecture is engaged by its users," are of paramount importance to budding self-builders. FAT are rescuing architecture from the grip of elitist intellectuals and encouraging everyone to have a go.

The group take a cut and paste approach to architecture by collaborating with practitioners of fine art, pop culture, and communication technology. This serves to blur the boundary between the different visual disciplines and deliver architecture to a broader audience. FAT's working methods are inclusive and imply that collaboration, rather than the mandate of a creative genius, is the key to propelling innovation in architecture.

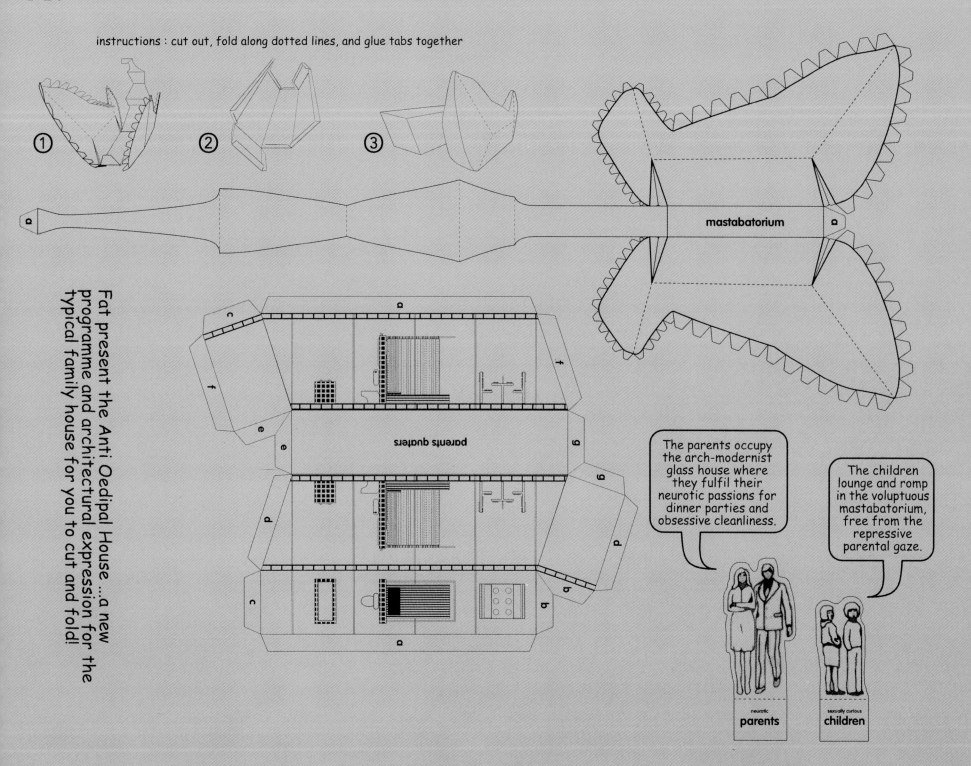

instructions : cut out, fold along dotted lines, and glue tabs together

① ② ③

mastabatorium

Fat present the Anti Oedipal House ...a new programme and architectural expression for the typical family house for you to cut and fold!

parents quaters

The parents occupy the arch-modernist glass house where they fulfil their neurotic passions for dinner parties and obsessive cleanliness.

The children lounge and romp in the voluptuous mastabatorium, free from the repressive parental gaze.

neurotic **parents**

sexually curious **children**

ROBERT BRUNO

steel HOUSE, ransom canyon, Lubbock, texas, USA, 1978–2002

Robert Bruno, lives and works in Lubbock, Texas, USA

One of the most radical aspects of Robert Bruno's self-built home is that it is made entirely of steel, a blunt and physically demanding material more commonly associated with sculpture or the frames of skyscrapers than the skin of a domestic home. In response to a housing industry mired in the production of flimsy, dry-walled squares, Bruno has taken the matter of shelter into his own hands, blatantly emphasizing fantasy over practical assembly.

Treating his material as though it were a pliable sheet of paper, Bruno single-handedly cut, folded, and welded together more than one hundred tons of steel plate into an edifice both organic and orgiastic. Since steel does not come in prefabricated elements, the house has been quite literally molded into being, resulting in a conspicuous lack of right angles. Unusually shaped walls and windows abound, evoking images from the natural world as diverse as eyelids, reptilian scales, plant stems, and arthropods. At the same time, soaring arcs and vaults refer to the romantic, man-made, Gothic cathedrals of yore, lending the home a spiritualism not typically found in the 'burbs. And while organicism is a trait Bruno's home shares with Greg Lynn's *Embryologic House* (p. 160) or Doug Garofalo's *Manilow Residence* (p. 36), in his version, imagined shapes travel from mind to hand without the mediation of a computer software program.

In a fascinating cross-pollination of early twentieth-century visionary thinking and contemporary special effects, Bruno conjures up images of back-to-the-future utopias as much as the jointed armor of Robocop. His home is a clear, uncompromised alternative to the two-car garage, built-in cabinet, show homes that developers would have us think are rife with aesthetic and psychological experience. Yet, ironically for Bruno, the desire to live apart meant making do with a conventional Ranch-style home until his dream world—constructed for one-third of the cost of a manufactured home—was complete.

ROBERT BRUNO, lives and works in Lubbock, TEXAS, USA

SARAH WIGGLESWORTH ARCHITECTS

9 stock orchard street, London, England, 2001

OPPOSITE THE FRONT GATE IS AN UNUSUAL COMBINATION OF MEDIEVAL AND INDUSTRIAL MATERIALS. ABOVE IT STANDS THE QUILTED WALL OF THE ARCHITECT'S OFFICE.

TOP LEFT THE INTERIOR OF THE LIBRARY TOWER IS LINED WITH BOOKSHELVES AND THE STAIRCASE, WHICH LEADS TO A SMALL RETREAT, HARBORS REST STOPS MARKED BY THE OCCASIONAL CUSHION.

TOP CENTER AND RIGHT THE PANTRY AND KITCHEN ARE LOCATED BEHIND PROJECTING STEEL FINS, WHICH PROVIDE AN AREA OF SHADE IN A GLAZED WALL THAT IS DESIGNED TO MAKE THE MOST OF NATURAL LIGHT.

standing at the threshold of *9 stock orchard street* is a gate fabricated with the unusual combination of willow and galvanized steel. It establishes a pattern for the whole building, which is a mixture of medieval and industrial technologies, or as wigglesworth herself describes it, "the slick and the hairy."

The project is alive with ideas as to how houses could be built. wigglesworth and her team have raided the techniques of other disciplines—many never before used in an urban setting—and dragged them to the attention of the architectural establishment. The use of straw-bale walls is a revolutionary technique for an inner-city building, a method that the architect is developing for the self-build market. straw bales are simple to build with and have high insulation properties. They are also sustainable, being made from a surplus, inexpensive material. The interior of the straw-bale wall is coated in lime for fireproofing but on the outside the straw is protected from the elements by corrugated

sheeting. In parts, this casing is made of transparent polycarbonate to expose the raggedness of the straw bales beneath.

wigglesworth intends *9 stock orchard street* to develop and mature continually. The sacks used in the building's sandbag wall are filled with a mixture of sand, cement, and lime. The sack cloth will disintegrate with the passing of time and the contents will seep out and harden to form what the architect describes as "a rippling wall of concrete."

9 stock orchard street is not only provocative in its use of materials and techniques, but also in the architectural styles applied to the different domestic and working quarters. The architect questions the common assumption that an office has to be hard and shiny by wrapping the studio space in a soft and cushioned fabric. This button-down quilt serves to dampen the noise of passing trains on the nearby railway line and adds another rich texture to a remarkably tactile building.

TOP ROW THE JUXTAPOSITION OF THE "SLICK AND THE HAIRY" IS CLEARLY ILLUSTRATED BY SMOOTH, TRANSPARENT SHEETING, WHICH EXPOSES THE RAGGED TEXTURE OF THE STRAW-BALE WALL BENEATH.

BOTTOM LEFT A SANDBAG WALL STANDS ABOVE HEFTY SUPPORTS THAT ARE CREATED BY PACKING WIRE CAGES CALLED "GABIONS" WITH CHUNKS OF RECYCLED CONCRETE.

BOTTOM RIGHT THE SANDBAG WALL WAS INSPIRED BY A PICTURE OF A COFFEE HOUSE THAT WAS FORTIFIED BY A WALL OF SANDBAGS DURING WORLD WAR II.

sarah wigglesworth architects, London, England

GAROFALO ARCHITECTS

Markow Residence, Prospect Heights, Illinois, USA, 1996–98
Manilow Residence, Burlington, Wisconsin, USA, currently under construction

TOP LEFT *MARKOW RESIDENCE.* GAROFALO ARCHITECTS GAVE THIS TRADITIONAL, SPLIT-LEVEL HOUSE A NEW "SKIN" WHICH BULGES AWAY FROM THE ORIGINAL FACADE ACCORDING TO THE RADICAL RESTRUCTURING WITHIN.

TOP RIGHT THE BACKSIDE OF THE HOME IS A FRENETIC COLLISION OF THE HOME'S ORIGINAL WINGS WITH A NEW SECOND STORY AND ROOF.

BOTTOM DETAIL OF SIDE.

OPPOSITE EXPLODED SECTION ILLUSTRATING HOW GAROFALO'S ADDITION SLICES INTO AND GRAFTS ONTO THE EXISTING STRUCTURE.

DOUG Garofalo's belief in an architecture of variation and difference is redefining the world of home improvement. By conventional measures of taste, his firm's extension of the *Markow Residence,* an existing postwar prefab in the Chicago suburb of Prospect Heights, is a DIY project gone terribly wrong. It doesn't follow any of the rules outlined in the home and garden magazines or on the television programs. The ad hoc second story is completely out of kilter with its well-balanced host and its jagged roofline abuts the original one to dizzying effects. However, the new, frenetic exterior is not only intentional but the result of a rigorous program of interior reconfigurations that respond to a close reading of the home's present circumstances and use.

When the first American suburbs began sprouting up in the 1940s, both architectural and social homogeneity were taken for granted. In Levittown, Long Island (the quintessential model), where 17,447 homes were built, only two "traditional" styles were available to home buyers: Cape Cod or Ranch.

This stylistic harmony was reinforced and even desired by the community's mostly white residents who were similar in age, stage in life cycle, and social standing. With twenty-first-century globalization and shifting populations, the American suburb has exploded with ethnic and cultural difference—and Garofalo is responding with innovative, often humorous, home additions that reflect the tastes and interests of diverse suburbanites for whom vernacular styling represents an old-world mentality.

For the split-level tract home of Polish-born Markow, Garofalo radically departed from the original's cubic division of space by grafting an open-plan scheme onto it. This opened up the tiny box-like living room into a soaring two-story public area with a catwalk leading to a study. It also made way for an expressionistic exploration of forms, including a rounded, green cell that contains the laundry room and childrens' bath. On all sides, the home is alive with abstract shapes and irregular windows in unlikely places and devoid of a final, unified order.

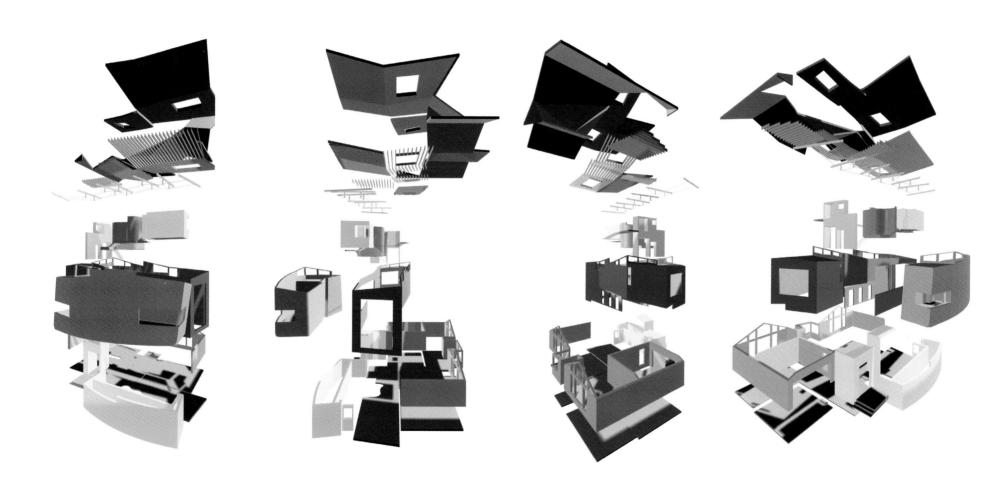

TOP *MANILOW RESIDENCE.* THE UNDULATING EXTENSION IS ONE OF A SERIES OF ADDITIONS TO A FORMER FARMHOUSE THAT IS NOW USED AS A RETREAT FROM THE CITY. THE FINISHED SITE WILL HAVE A RANGE OF QUALITIES "THAT EMBRACE ANIMATED GATHERINGS AS WELL AS MOMENTS OF SOLITUDE."

BOTTOM AND OPPOSITE THE EXTREME, FLOOR-TO-CEILING CURVILINEAR FORMS WOULD MAKE MOST GENERAL CONTRACTORS RAISE THEIR EYEBROWS, SO GAROFALO WORKED WITH A CABINETRY FABRICATING COMPANY WHO CONVERTED THE SHAPES INTO ENTITIES THEIR SOFTWARE COULD UNDERSTAND.

At the *Manilow Residence* in Wisconsin, Garofalo has pushed the limits of acceptable home improvement even more left of center in his expansion of a farmhouse for a large, extended family. Using Maya, an animation software popular among Hollywood filmmakers, Garofalo created an organic, undulating channel that attaches to the quaint original house like a feeding tube or parasite. The program allows him to transfer the drawing into precisely cut, laminated, plywood beams that hook onto the home on many sides, sculpting it into a form more in tune with the rolling landscape. The update breathes new life into the original by lending it a much-desired personality and theatricality. As with the *Markow Residence*, the overall scheme is loosely programmed and amenable, demonstrating Garofalo's overarching concern that the built environment "promot[e] networks more than objects, processes and performances more than monumental presences...."

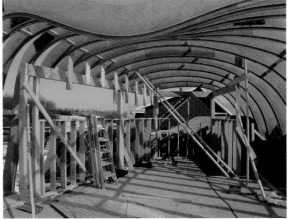

Garofalo Architects, Chicago, Illinois, USA

MICHAEL HOENES

tin-can houses, lesotho, south africa, 1991 & ongoing

TOP EACH CAN IS PIERCED FOUR TIMES AND WIRED TOGETHER HORIZONTALLY. VERTICAL WIRES ARE WOVEN TOGETHER IN THE GAPS AT INTERVALS OF THREE. BECAUSE OF THE HOLLOW SPACE OF AIR INSIDE EACH CAN, THE FINISHED WALLS ARE THERMALLY INSULATING.

RIGHT A LAYER OF CANS FIXED IN PLACE WITH CEMENT FORMS THE BASE FOR EACH MODULE.

BOTTOM IN ADDITION TO PRIVATE HOMES, THE SYSTEM IS ALSO BEING EMPLOYED TO CONSTRUCT BUSINESSES.

In the opening sequence of jamie uys' 1981 film *the gods must be crazy*, a pilot flying over the kalahari desert carelessly drops a coca-cola bottle from the window of his plane. retrieved by a junt-wasi tribesman, the bottle instantly turns his world upside-down as the members of his formerly peaceful family fight amongst themselves for ownership of the sleek container. ironically, twenty years after this fictional but cautionary tale of western incursion into intact cultures, coca-cola (along with other brands of soda) is making a positive architectural contribution in africa thanks to its tin-can packaging and a little german engineering.

It all started in 1991 when michael hoenes, a stuttgart student of mechanical engineering, visited south africa. inspired by native children's toys made of twisted wire, he developed a fireplace of tin cans held together with wire to take back to europe with him as part of his studies. after building the hearth, it became apparent that a stool and table were needed to enjoy it, which he also constructed out of cans. soon neighbors began asking about shelters to protect their watchdogs, quickly becoming avid fans of hoenes' tin-can doghouses. in 1996, when a woman requested a hut for her guard, hoenes' concept took off among the locals.

Although the shack measured only fifty square feet—enough for a tin-can bed—the guard was so pleased that he expanded it and moved in his family of five.

Today the basic one-room module is easily produced and assembled by anyone. the cans are cleaned, punctured, and then strung together horizontally and vertically with wire, lending the walls an elastic quality that can withstand tension and pressure. once erected, the interior room is lined with board panels, which may be decorated in any manner. the houses sit on simple pieces of chipboard, which have been made watertight and warm by foundations of cans fixed with cement and covered with foil.

In africa, the finished homes are typically coated with deep red, anticorrosion paint whose hue is not unlike what might be found on a ranch home on the west coast of america. however, when a cluster of the houses made their debut at expo 2000 in hanover, germany, the cans were left exposed to satisfy the expectations of a western audience. in an overdue turnaround of circumstances, it was citizens of the west who eagerly clamored around to learn from strange and shiny curiosities from afar.

michael hoenes, lives and works in south africa

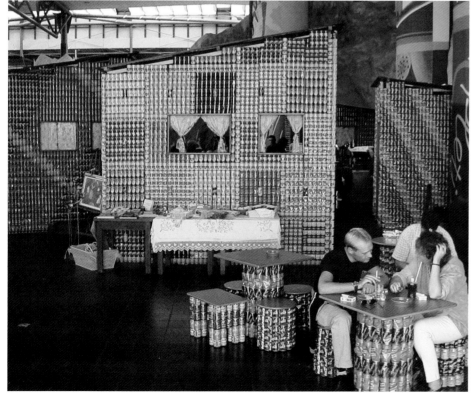

TOP LEFT WORKERS ASSEMBLE INDIVIDUAL WALL SEGMENTS INTO A FINISHED HOME.

TOP RIGHT EACH HOME COSTS ABOUT $800 TO CONSTRUCT, A QUARTER OF WHAT IT COSTS TO THE BUILD A COMPARABLE, BUT LESS WELL-INSULATED HOME MADE OF CONCRETE BLOCKS.

BOTTOM A VILLAGE OF THE *TIN-CAN HOMES* WAS CONSTRUCTED IN THE AFRICA HALL AT EXPO 2000 IN HANOVER, GERMANY.

MARJETICA POTRC

east wahdat upgrading program, Museum Moderner Kunst, Vienna, Austria, 2001

BOTTOM POTRC RECONSTRUCTS EXAMPLES OF HOMES BUILT AS PART OF THE *EAST WAHDAT UPGRADING PROGRAM*, AMMAN, JORDAN.

Marjetica Potrc is an artist and architect who reinterprets designs of real working homes in the form of gallery installations. often these homes are based on individual housing initiatives taken from self-build schemes found in shantytowns all over the world. Her work looks at the failures of town planning and highlights situations where the members of an improvised community have taken the development of their district into their own hands.

shantytowns are a common development around city fringes the world over. These unregulated and improvised settlements form a large proportion of the world's housing. In an interview with Hans Ulrich Obrist, Potrc states that, "Twenty years ago, shantytowns were not even drawn into city plans. The planners thought that they could just erase them and relocate the population to public housing. Today, it is known that inhabitants don't necessarily want to move to such housing. shantytowns can be upgraded and be functional communities." one example of this is the *East wahdat upgrading program*, which Potrc recreated at the Museum Moderner Kunst, vienna, Austria.

During the 1980s in Amman, Jordan, around a quarter of all new housing took the form of shanty dwellings. A typical response to such a situation would be to bulldoze the site and force the squatter community to move elsewhere. In Amman, however, the residents of East wahdat were given the opportunity to build their own homes around a core unit supplying electricity and clean water. Each resident was given a plot of land while the Urban Development Department provided road access, electricity, water, and a sewage system. Neighbors helped each other move their existing shanty structures to the corner of each lot and these were then used as temporary shelters while the first room of each home was built, and later moved into.

Potrc communicates the success of this program by re-creating examples of the self-built homes in the context of an art gallery. The result of the program in East wahdat is a refreshing alternative to the formality of concrete tower blocks, where similar fluctuating populations can sometimes be housed. The homes are the inhabitants' own creations and can be altered at will. This is in stark contrast to the usual mass housing programs, whereby a person far removed from the situation of the end user designs the homogeneous dwellings.

Marjetica Potrc, lives and works in Ljubljana, slovenia

KOEPPEL & MARTINEZ

schlafhaus (house for sleeping), asturias, navia, spain, 1998–2002

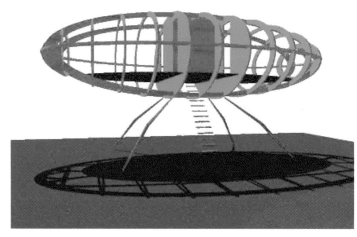

aerodynamic is the adjective that springs to mind when describing koeppel & martinez's schlafhaus, a home expansion project that employs zeppelin technology, is constructed like a model airplane, and looks like a ufo.

modeled on its airborn cousin, the dirigible, schlafhaus is a cigar-shaped pod consisting of a lightweight wooden skeleton wrapped with a flexible skin (in this case, cotton). whereas the blimp was designed to be kept aloft, schlafhaus is decidedly grounded by four steel legs and a hard outer shell. as with toy planes, the illusion of flight is maintained by several coats of translucent lacquer, which harden and stabilize the otherwise easily damaged membrane. a final coat of aluminum varnish blocks damaging uv rays and gives the house a streamlined, alien appearance.

designed for a pair of spanish artists who live and work in an old rural mill, schlafhaus is an of-the-moment, as-permanent-as-you-want-it extension of their personal living space. true to its name, it is used principally for sleeping and contains only two bedrooms, a bath, and an entryway.

separate sleeping quarters are nothing new, especially in warm regions where screened-in porches or pitched tents provide relief on steamy summer nights. in this instance, koeppel & martinez have updated the options with artistic imagination and affordable structural invention.

AMERICAN INGENUITY INC.

Geodesic Dome Homes, various locations, 1976 & ongoing

OPPOSITE AN EXAMPLE OF ONE OF OVER FIFTY STOCK FLOOR PLANS FROM WHICH A DOME HOME CAN BE CREATED.

THIS PAGE THE DOME ARRIVES AS A SERIES OF TRIANGULAR PANELS IN THE FORM OF A SELF-ASSEMBLY KIT. THE PANELS ARE MADE FROM A MIXTURE OF CONCRETE AND STEEL FOR STRENGTH AND DURABILITY. THE SEAMS BETWEEN THE PANELS ARE SEALED TO COMPLETE THE TOUGH CONCRETE SHELL, WHICH IS ENERGY EFFICIENT AND LOW MAINTENANCE.

self-assembly homes are nothing new. what distinguishes the American Ingenuity construction kit from others available is that it's based on the principle of Buckminster Fuller's geodesic dome, an approximate sphere made with a framework of triangles and hexagons.

During the 1960s, numerous American counterculture groups embraced the geodesic dome. Its distinctive form became a symbol for those who rejected the square houses of suburbia to establish hippy communes, often in the deserts of the western united states. Perhaps the most fascinating aspect of American Ingenuity is how this once radical approach to domestic architecture has been repackaged to suit the regular midwestern family with an appetite for DIY, just the sort of people the counterculture movement was reacting against.

Dropouts in the 1960s used the geodesic dome to conduct an all out assault on the typical suburban home. In a bizarre cross fertilization of ideas, those same revolutionary building techniques are now being sold as an extension to the massive range of DIY products available in any large home improvement store.

The geodesic structure of the American Ingenuity system is self-supporting, energy efficient, and inherently strong. The dome builder is able to create the home they want, where they want it, and how they want it, providing it fits into the flexible pattern of the geodesic frame. However, this approach appears to be a little too left field for some of the dome owners. Those who are not quite ready to fully embrace dome living can disguise the unusual shape of their homes by adding elements to make them look more like regular houses. such alterations to the dome's facade also ensure that it will not upset any conservative neighbors. However, should a hurricane hit their community, the dome owners' homes would stand firm while their neighbors' regular dwellings would be left in dire need of repair.

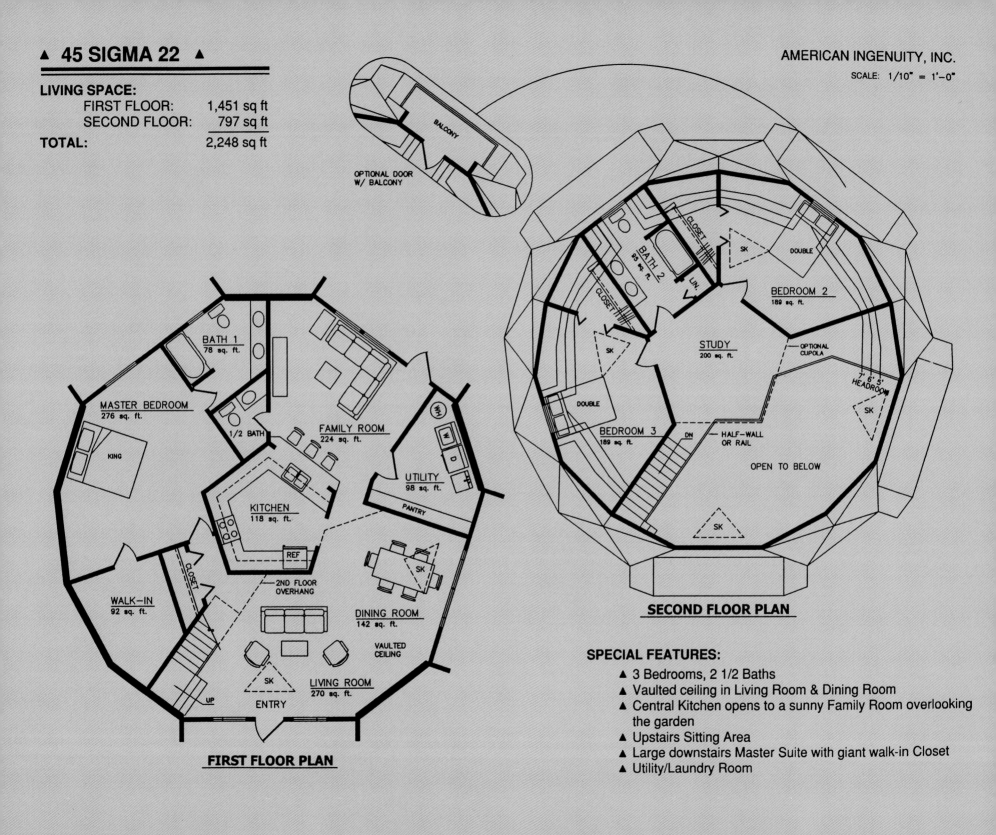

▲ 45 SIGMA 22 ▲

LIVING SPACE:
FIRST FLOOR: 1,451 sq ft
SECOND FLOOR: 797 sq ft

TOTAL: 2,248 sq ft

AMERICAN INGENUITY, INC.
SCALE: 1/10" = 1'-0"

OPTIONAL DOOR
W/ BALCONY

BALCONY

BATH 1
78 sq. ft.

MASTER BEDROOM
276 sq. ft.

KING

1/2 BATH

FAMILY ROOM
224 sq. ft.

UTILITY
98 sq. ft.

WH

W
D

KITCHEN
118 sq. ft.

PANTRY

REF

WALK-IN
92 sq. ft.

CLOSET

2ND FLOOR
OVERHANG

DINING ROOM
142 sq. ft.

SK

VAULTED
CEILING

UP

SK

ENTRY

LIVING ROOM
270 sq. ft.

FIRST FLOOR PLAN

CLOSET

BATH 2
93 sq. ft.

SK

DOUBLE

CLOSET

UP

BEDROOM 2
189 sq. ft.

STUDY
200 sq. ft.

OPTIONAL
CUPOLA

7' 6" 5'
HEADROOM

DOUBLE

BEDROOM 3
189 sq. ft.

DN

HALF—WALL
OR RAIL

SK

OPEN TO BELOW

SK

SECOND FLOOR PLAN

SPECIAL FEATURES:

▲ 3 Bedrooms, 2 1/2 Baths
▲ Vaulted ceiling in Living Room & Dining Room
▲ Central Kitchen opens to a sunny Family Room overlooking the garden
▲ Upstairs Sitting Area
▲ Large downstairs Master Suite with giant walk-in Closet
▲ Utility/Laundry Room

▲ KIT OPTIONS INCLUDED IN PLANS ▲

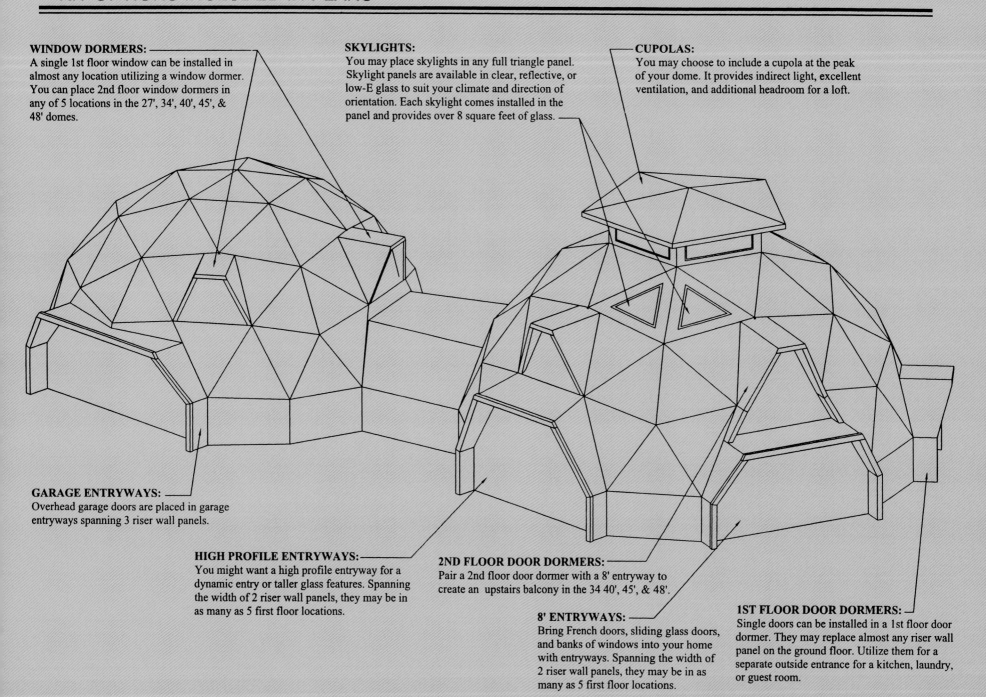

WINDOW DORMERS:
A single 1st floor window can be installed in almost any location utilizing a window dormer. You can place 2nd floor window dormers in any of 5 locations in the 27', 34', 40', 45', & 48' domes.

SKYLIGHTS:
You may place skylights in any full triangle panel. Skylight panels are available in clear, reflective, or low-E glass to suit your climate and direction of orientation. Each skylight comes installed in the panel and provides over 8 square feet of glass.

CUPOLAS:
You may choose to include a cupola at the peak of your dome. It provides indirect light, excellent ventilation, and additional headroom for a loft.

GARAGE ENTRYWAYS:
Overhead garage doors are placed in garage entryways spanning 3 riser wall panels.

HIGH PROFILE ENTRYWAYS:
You might want a high profile entryway for a dynamic entry or taller glass features. Spanning the width of 2 riser wall panels, they may be in as many as 5 first floor locations.

2ND FLOOR DOOR DORMERS:
Pair a 2nd floor door dormer with a 8' entryway to create an upstairs balcony in the 34 40', 45', & 48'.

8' ENTRYWAYS:
Bring French doors, sliding glass doors, and banks of windows into your home with entryways. Spanning the width of 2 riser wall panels, they may be in as many as 5 first floor locations.

1ST FLOOR DOOR DORMERS:
Single doors can be installed in a 1st floor door dormer. They may replace almost any riser wall panel on the ground floor. Utilize them for a separate outside entrance for a kitchen, laundry, or guest room.

American Ingenuity Inc., Rockledge, Florida, USA

BRIGGS PORT-A-FOLD LTD.

Port-A-Fold shelter system, 2002

OPPOSITE THE MULTIPURPOSE SHELTER IS DESIGNED FOR EASY TRANSPORT, HANDLING, AND ASSEMBLY. IT MAY BE USED OVER AND OVER FOR DIFFERENT APPLICATIONS WHICH REDUCES THE INITIAL INVESTMENT, COMPARED TO FIXED STRUCTURES.

TOP THE SHELTER SHIPS FLAT BUT CAN BE POPPED INTO PLACE BY FOUR PEOPLE IN APPROXIMATELY FIFTEEN MINUTES.

A pop-up metal box assembled in fifteen minutes is not what typically comes to mind when speaking of a "home" proper. But, increasingly, shelters such as the *Port-A-Fold are* home to thousands of people who have been displaced by war, natural disasters, or over-population.

Boasting "simplicity in design," the *Port-A-Fold* is a collapsible, hard-walled box—with a built-in door and window—whose polystyrene panels are faced with prepainted, embossed aluminum or steel and edged with PVC channels. A unique hinge system allows four people to fold the one-piece structure into a fifteen-inch-high, flat rectangle for shipping and then expand it again once on site. The shelter is so slim and lightweight that fifteen units can easily be transported in a standard shipping container at one time.

Already in use as disaster relief enclosures, refugee shelters, and field clinics, the *Port-A-Fold's* industrial common sense and know-how is simply waiting to be transported into the realm of accepted domestic architecture.

On a practical level, the *Port-A-Fold's* standard equipment is what most prospective homeowners, as well as mortgage banks and insurance companies, seek out in potential dwellings: durable construction, fireproof and watertight materials, and good insulation (not to mention that the *Port-A-Fold* is sterile, easy to clean, and made of recycled materials whenever possible). Theoretically speaking, architects and designers have been appropriating concepts from the commercial sector since the early twentieth century. Without the balloon frame, the Ranch-style house would never have evolved. Without the steel-frame skyscraper, high-rise apartments would still be hypothetical.

While the idea of growing old in what appears to be a sterile white box may be daunting to some, the fact remains that most suburban homes—and mobile homes, too, for that matter—are little more than conglomerations of square, white rooms with doors and windows in need of a human touch. With a little decoration and some periodic home improvement—you can add on modules endlessly—the *Port-A-Fold* could go a long way in supplying people of all walks of life with smart, low-cost housing.

BRIGGS PORT-A-FOLD Ltd., USA

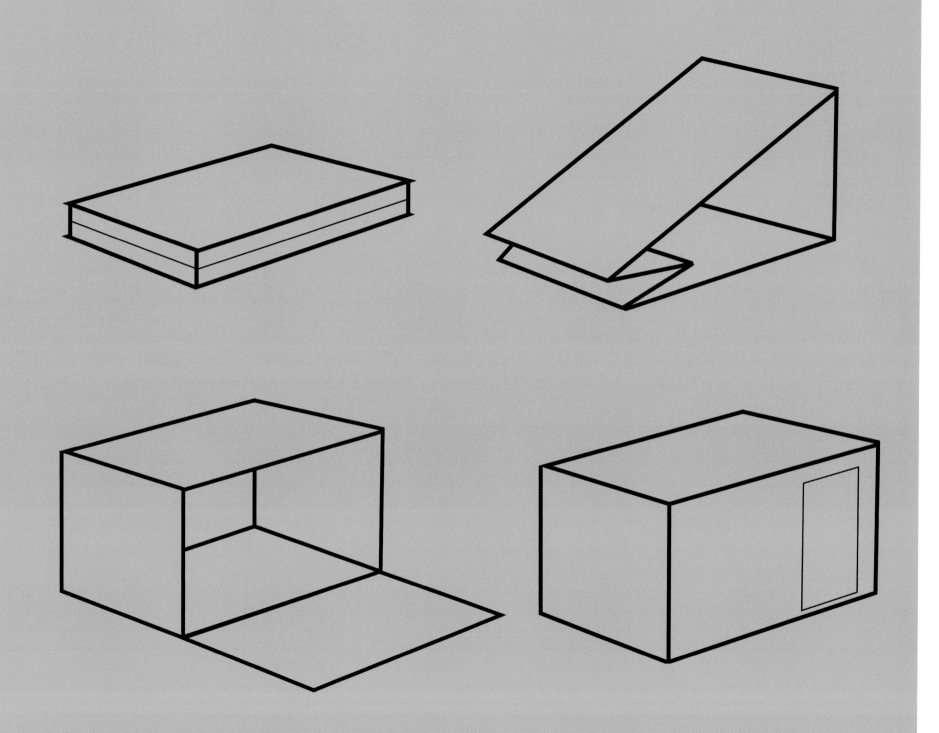

JESSICA STOCKHOLDER & OPENOFFICE

Houses x Artists, 1998 & ongoing

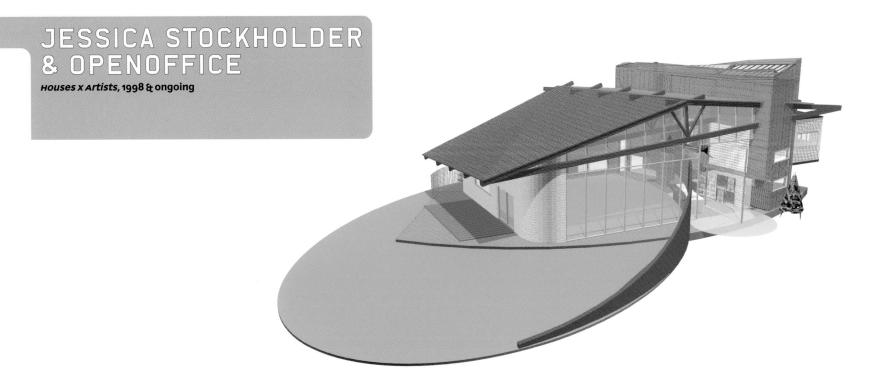

TOP STOCKHOLDER EMPLOYS THE TYPICAL, SMALL-HOUSE CONVENTION OF A SINGLE WET WALL FOR HER HOME'S STRUCTURAL CORE. USUALLY A MINOR ELEMENT IN A HOME'S CONSTRUCTION, HERE IT PLAYS A CENTRAL PHYSICAL AND AESTHETIC ROLE.

RIGHT AND OPPOSITE SCALE MODEL OF THE HOUSE (2 INCHES = 1 FOOT) MADE OF EVERYDAY MATERIALS WHICH SIMULATE THE COLOR AND MATERIAL SUGGESTED FOR THE DESIGN. THE MODEL ACTS AS A LARGE DOLLHOUSE WITH WHICH VIEWERS CAN ENGAGE VISUALLY AND PHYSICALLY.

OPPOSITE BOTTOM THE HOME'S BEDROOM IS A READY-MADE HOUSE TRAILER WHICH CANTILEVERS OUT FROM THE WET WALL.

suburban homes are almost without exception ugly, bland, or both because they are based on a manufacturer's standard. By thinking pictorially and arranging space sculpturally, however, artist Jessica Stockholder demonstrates that the terms "funky" or even "pretty" can rightfully apply to tract homes.

Beginning in 1998, the New York-based collaborative openoffice invited a variety of artists to design residential homes with one stipulation: that each proposal result in a house that could actually be built. In keeping with her own artwork, Stockholder responded with a concept that is informed as much by sculpture and painting as it is by architecture. Crossing the boundaries of all three disciplines, Stockholder typically combines colored paint with found objects—from lamps to chairs to wooden planks—into three-dimensional objects and room installations that appear to have been arranged compositionally.

For her housing proposal, she simply transferred this sensibility to a much larger scale, combining a found trailer home, a surfboard, and bits of Baroque furniture with a lively lime green wall, ruddy roof, and aqua floor. In her assemblage, the camper becomes a bedroom, the surfboard acts as a stair

railing, and the Baroque furniture is used to face the kitchen cabinets. The home is akin to one of her room installations, a wild and free intermingling of emotive color and personal forms. Her painterly touch is most apparent in the pastel pink wet wall, which contains all of the plumbing, electricity, and appliances in its concrete mass. The cast-in-pace monolith is the main structural element of the home and supports a bivouacked, lean-to roof, a stairwell, a nested bathroom, a suspended private wing, and a fireplace. However, Stockholder has played down its serious role with a sugary hue that is more reminiscent of bubble gum. This is also true of the sweeping, purple garden wall that originates inside the house and extends into the yard in a manner resembling a brush stroke and sculptural arc. While distinctly functional, the broad curve also calls to mind the vivid colors and shapes of playground furniture.

Stockholder seeks to establish "new territory for cultural expansion and civic reclamation" by approaching the private house as an eclectic montage of both prefabricated elements and personal *tchotchkes* rather than as a programmatic grid—a strategy of contemporary relevance to developers and aspiring self-builders alike.

Jessica Stockholder, lives and works in New Haven, Connecticut, USA

RICHARD J. L. MARTIN

global peace containers, cross keys, jamaica, 2000 & ongoing

OPPOSITE TOP THE DELIVERY, UNLOADING, AND POSITIONING OF FOUR FREIGHT CONTAINERS AT THE CROSS KEYS SITE, WHERE A FOUNDATION IS PREPARED BY THE LOCAL RESIDENTS.

OPPOSITE BOTTOM LOUVERED WINDOWS ARE CUT INTO THE CONTAINER WALLS AND A PITCHED ROOF IS INSTALLED TO SHELTER THE INNER COURTYARD.

RIGHT PLANS OF THE FINISHED FREIGHT CONTAINER HOMES. THE CONTAINERS ARE ARRANGED TO FORM A SPACIOUS COMMON AREA AT THE CENTER OF THE HOME.

shipping containers are designed to be durable and as a consequence are difficult to dispose of. The team behind the *global peace containers* initiative has breathed new life into such crates by converting them into homes and other facilities for a community in Jamaica. The scheme addresses two major problems: an excess of industrial waste in the First world and an immediate need for shelter in the Third world.

The people housed by this project are encouraged to take an active role in the construction of their homes. The modifications needed to renovate the freight containers are relatively straightforward. This factor means that the inhabitants are empowered to create their own homes, while also learning new and worthwhile skills. However, the prime modification that has to occur is to fill the crates with sentimental content. Prior to this act the container can still be viewed as a functional object used to transport goods around the world. But unload the freight and replace it with an individual, a group, or a family and the crate suddenly becomes a home. To a worker in a Third world sweatshop the freight container can be seen as a box that carries the product of his cheap labor to the department stores of the First world. Now he

might look on that same container as his future home.

This mode of thought has much in common with the ideas presented by FAT (p. 22). They suggest that the Modernist-style house has become a status symbol of First world luxury. All ornamental detailing is usually stripped away in the creation of such a dwelling. This is in direct opposition to the methods used in the *global peace containers* scheme. *global peace containers* take the shipping crates, which are essentially functional objects devoid of any decoration, and adorn them with emotion, experience, and feeling to make a home.

Richard J. L. Martin, Atlanta, Georgia, USA

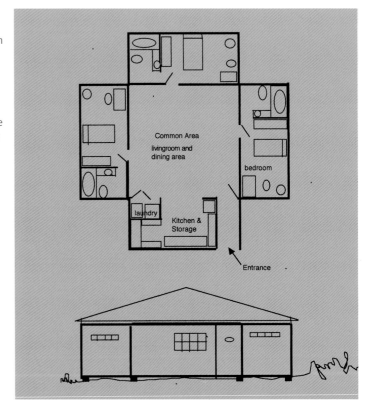

VITO ACCONCI

House of cars #2, private collection, USA, 1988

RIGHT EACH CAR UNIT IS A SPECIFIC LIVING AREA. AT ONE END OF THE COMPLEX IS A KITCHEN, AT THE OTHER A COMBINATION BEDROOM AND BATH.

OPPOSITE MEASURING 35 X 16 X 13 FEET, THE HOUSE IS MADE OF JUNK CARS, WHICH ARE PRESERVED BY ZINC COATING AND CROWNED WITH A FLICKER SIGN THAT READS "LIVE OUT OF THIS WORLD." IT IS POSSIBLE TO WALK THROUGH THE MIDDLE OF ONE CAR UNIT UP THE STAIRS THROUGH THE CENTER UNIT AND DOWN AGAIN THROUGH THE THIRD UNIT.

cars are nothing less than rolling boxes whose roofs, panels, doors, and windows mimic the architecture of our domestic homes. yet unlike permanent abodes, autos are more immediate visual signifiers of our notoriously fickle tastes and are thus upgraded and "improved" by the industry with the frequency of a fashion collection. with a social obsolescence of roughly six years—the average resale period—cars continue to be one of the First world's most expendable products.

It was exactly this aesthetic of impermanence that endeared the American automobile to postwar POP artists on both sides of the Atlantic, but for artists of the succeeding generation—such as vito ACCONCI—who inherited the heaped junkyards and lived through the oil crisis, obsolescence took on greater social implications. Today, with international attention focused on the KYOTO Protocol, the problem of what to do with towering masses of vehicles past their time and prime has never been more urgent.

vito ACCONCI turned the once-rolling

homes into parodies of their static cousins. His *House of cars #2* comprises six, hollowed-out auto bodies stacked in twos within an I-beam framework reminiscent of suburban peaked-roofed homes. All three units have conventional, eight-foot ceilings and are outfitted with basic amenities made from boat appliances. on one end is a kitchen with a stove, sink, and refrigerator packed into the double trunk. on the other is a bedroom and bath containing a sling-like bed of woven steel wire in the trunk and a sink, shower, and toilet under the hood. The raised middle unit serves as a porch and living room.

Just as domestic architecture has influenced the size, shape, and accessories of our cars over the last century, so *House of cars #2* is an innovative example of the inverse. A sign wedged into the hood over the home's living room reads "Live out of This world." whether interpreted literally or metaphorically, the imperative urges us all to consider how we might live beyond a manufacturer's expiration date.

vito ACCONCI, lives and works in Brooklyn, NEW YORK, USA

CHAPTER 2

MOVE TO THE STICKS

Are the smell and noise of the big city starting to bug you? Get outta town! The houses in this section harmonize with nature so they won't spoil the view for city folk who want to come and look at trees and sheep on a sunday afternoon.

The majority of projects featured in "Move to the sticks" look to the countryside as an escape from the noise and smell of the city. Not because the country is free from noise and smell—far from it—but because its remoteness offers freedom from the order of the city. Living in an urban location usually means conforming to a grid and relying on the state or a utility company for the provision of energy and waste disposal. For *Earthship* and *Monolithic Dome* dwellers, the services provided by the grid are far from satisfactory and rather than comply with it, they reject it outright, choosing instead to fend for themselves.

The natural environment provides a situation to try out new ways of living that would not be possible in ordered, industrial cities. The homes presented in this chapter explore alternative solutions to finding a home in the country. These dwellings try their best to work in harmony with their location and whether it's the desert, a forest, or coral reef, the houses are designed for minimal impact. Some achieve this by either hovering among the trees, as in Dawson Brown Architecture's *"Tree House" studio Pavilion*, Softroom's *Tree House*, and Lacaton & Vassal's *Individual House* or floating on water as in Jean-Michel Ducanelle's *Les Anthenea* and Herman Hertzberger's *watervilla* and *semi-waterhouses*.

Trying to build a home on a virgin, rural site, in the UK at least, is fraught with complications. Rarely is permission granted to build on such sites and planning authorities seem especially hostile to any building that is not in keeping with a traditional style. Jonathan Bell, writing in *Blueprint,* remarks that "Neoclassicists, whatever their rank, rarely have to struggle through the planning system, regardless of scale, grandeur, and competence."

In the same magazine, James Heartfield writes, "since the 1970s, the historic population shift from country to town has been reversed." It appears that the smell and noise of the big city is proving too much for some urban dwellers, and the growing use of the Internet means fewer people are restricted to living in a location dictated by their workplace.

What will happen when all these city folk descend upon the country? If thousands of them opt for a rural existence then it will force house prices up by a ridiculous margin. On the other hand, if thousands of new homes are built then there won't be any remaining countryside for all the other city folk to come and look at on a Sunday afternoon. Clearly there is a problem.

"You'll always find me out in the country" sang a jolly cliff Richard in 1966, but if sir cliff were to take up residence in one of the country retreats in this chapter, he could not guarantee that he'd always be found. Kas Oosterhuis' *Variomatic House*, for instance, can be camouflaged to disappear into any surroundings. The system employed relies on cladding the house in a pattern to suit the surrounding area, but other dwellings, like *Earthships*, are hidden by being buried in the ground. Dwellings such as Rural studio's *corrugated construction*, shigeru Ban's *Naked House*, and Lacaton & Vassal's *Minimum House* don't try to mask their existence, but their style is inconspicuous and unobtrusive. These examples acknowledge that the countryside, especially in smaller countries, is rarely an unspoiled rural idyll. The three homes resemble agricultural outbuildings and respect the countryside as an industrious working environment.

Moving to the sticks presents an opportunity to start afresh. The projects here demonstrate that it is not just about a simple way of life away from the city but a provocative existence that challenges the accepted norms of urban housing with real working alternative dwellings.

JEAN-MICHEL DUCANELLE

Les Anthenea, no fixed location, 2001

OPPOSITE AND FOLLOWING PAGES DETAILS OF THE *AQUASPHERE* SHOWING THE SUN DECK, UNDERWATER VIEWING WINDOW, AND THE CIRCULAR STYLING APPLIED TO THE LIVING AND SLEEPING QUARTERS.

TOP AN ARTIST'S IMPRESSION OF A BEACH RESORT FORMED BY ARRANGING A FLOTILLA OF *AQUASPHERE* CRAFT WITHIN A NETWORK OF FLOATING WALKWAYS.

The *Anthenea*, or *Aquasphere*, as it is also known, is a luxurious, spherical dwelling that floats on water. It was designed by French naval architect Jean-Michel Ducanelle in answer to a need for a floating habitation capsule to cater to a growing trade in ecotourism. The styling of the craft resembles a flying saucer and does not damage or disturb the fragile, underwater habitat of coral reefs. The pod-like shape rests delicately upon the water but is also stable and can be raised or lowered while in the sea by a system of inflatable floats. A wraparound, 360 degree window provides a panoramic view and looks over a circular flotation ring, which acts as a spacious, outdoor surface area.

The interior is compact but contains all the comforts of any luxury apartment, including Jacuzzi and cocktail bar, as well as the usual amenities of kitchen, air conditioning, and a home entertainment system. There is also a glass bottom, which opens the interior to the marine environment and features exterior illumination for viewing underwater life.

The *Anthenea's* design enables it to be hooked up to other *Aquasphere* craft to form whole floating communities. Ducanelle envisages beachside resorts made entirely of *Antheneas*. Such a flotilla might act as an extension to an existing small island and rule out the need to build on dry land. At the moment, the *Anthenea* is used primarily as recreational accommodation but it presents an incredibly attractive proposition for an alternative method of housing.

Jean-Michel Ducanelle, lives and works in France

SHIGERU BAN ARCHITECTS

Naked House (case study House 10E), Kawagoe, Saitama, Japan, 2001
Paper House, Yamanakako, Japan, 1995

OPPOSITE *PAPER HOUSE* AT DAY AND NIGHT. HERE, BAN WAS HEAVILY INFLUENCED BY MIES VAN DER ROHE'S *FARNSWORTH HOUSE* (P. 13).

TOP A VIEW FROM INSIDE *PAPER HOUSE* ILLUSTRATING THE CONTINUITY BETWEEN INTERIOR AND EXTERIOR SPACE.

FOLLOWING PAGES *NAKED HOUSE* AGAIN DEMONSTRATES BAN'S INTEREST IN CREATING OPEN, FLUID SPACES UNDER A LARGE, CONTINUOUS ROOF.

One of the most remarkable aspects of Shigeru Ban's work is his reworking of the traditional Japanese house with contemporary methods and materials. The exterior of *case study House 10E* is coated in translucent white sheets of plastic, which saturate the house with light during the day and cause it to glow like a lantern after dark. The house, however, does not intrude upon its location because it is camouflaged among the rice paddy fields by its similarity to a green house. Insulation is provided by an inner membrane, which is made from the same nylon fabric commonly used in the manufacture of tents. This skin-on-frame structure follows in a long tradition of domestic architecture in Japan and is reminiscent of the wood and paper constructions that date back hundreds of years.

Walls have never been regarded as a necessary structural element in traditional Japanese dwellings, as a strong wooden framework was sufficient to support the building. The introduction of movable screens to act as interior walls made the homes more flexible. With the exception of the bathroom there are no dividing walls inside *case study House 10E*. A series of portable box-like rooms on wheels serve as the sleeping quarters and update the movable partition screens. The mobile rooms can be hooked up to air conditioners or even pushed outside when the weather is warm. This interchange between the interior and exterior follows yet another Japanese tradition whereby the screen dividing the home and garden can be removed to establish an open living space.

The *Paper House* is an outstanding example of Shigeru Ban's commitment to experimentation with different materials. A line of paper tubes, similar to those used to roll carpets around, stand side by side in a looping formation on a 1,100-square-foot floor. The arrangement of the tubes creates a large circular space with a freestanding kitchen unit as the only incorporated facility. Light filters into this space through narrow gaps between the tubes. The tubes are protected from the elements by a series of movable, transparent screens that surround the perimeter of the house and open out onto a terrace overlooking a lake. Movable closets and sliding partitions render the space completely flexible, and the open terrace removes the barrier between exterior and interior living spaces.

In his earlier projects, Ban often used fabric screens as movable dividing walls, and it was the tubes on which this fabric was delivered that inspired his *Paper House*. While visiting a factory, Ban discovered that the tubes are inexpensive to produce in almost any length and diameter and are made from recycled paper. He collaborated with Professor Gengo Matsui to experiment further with the tubes as a structural material. The resulting technology was given the name "Paper Tube Structure (PTS)" and has appeared in much of Ban's recent work, from the luxurious lakeside *Paper House*, where the Japanese Ministry of construction first gave it their approval, to the basic relief shelters used to house victims of the Kobe earthquake.

DAWSON BROWN ARCHITECTURE

"tree house" studio pavilion, palm beach, new south wales, Australia, 1999

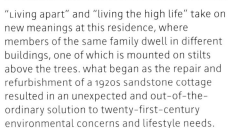

TOP THE FIRST FLOOR OF THE "TREE HOUSE" ADDITION CONTAINS A BEDROOM AND A BATHROOM, WHILE THE SECOND FLOOR IS USED AS A LIVING AREA THAT MAY BE CONVERTED INTO A GUEST ROOM.

BOTTOM RIGHT NORTH ELEVATION ILLUSTRATING HOW THE HOUSE BALANCES ON RADICAL, X-SHAPED LEGS WHICH ATTACH TO THE ROCK FACE BELOW.

OPPOSITE NO TREES WERE REMOVED IN THE CONSTRUCTION PROCESS, AND THE RESULTING HOME RESEMBLES A SCULPTURE IN THE FOREST, WHEN VIEWED FROM THE ORIGINAL COTTAGE.

"Living apart" and "living the high life" take on new meanings at this residence, where members of the same family dwell in different buildings, one of which is mounted on stilts above the trees. what began as the repair and refurbishment of a 1920s sandstone cottage resulted in an unexpected and out-of-the-ordinary solution to twenty-first-century environmental concerns and lifestyle needs.

originally constructed as a modest cabin in the mid-twentieth century, the tiny cottage was one of only six homes nestled into the native banksia trees on a remote peninsula overlooking the Pacific. Today, however, the home is not large enough to accommodate the spatial needs of its current owner, even as a vacation residence. expansion in some form was much desired but complicated by the fact that the cottage is a historic residence and the surrounding bush land a reserve.

Dawson Brown's solution was simple but revolutionary: integrate into nature by building skyward and underground. using natural timber, the firm constructed a soaring tree house that alludes to the style of the original

home but sits on radical, x-shaped, scissor-trussed legs attached to the rock cliff below. This detached bedroom/studio recedes into the trees and provides additional square footage without compromising the environment or the original cabin to which it is attached by a bridge spanning the swimming pool. Even more unconventional, the architects burrowed beneath the pool to carve out another new bedroom and bath which are illuminated with reflected light from a porthole in the pool wall.

Elevated structures are already commonplace in the urban jungle, whether train platforms or cranes, scaffolding or rock concert stages, so it was only a matter of time before they came to the country. In fact, the technique is already commonplace in other parts of the world— from native settlements to beachfront communities—where people rely on height to protect them from enemies, animals, or rising tides. yet in this instance, living high up allows the residents to be at one with nature with minimal impact to the site.

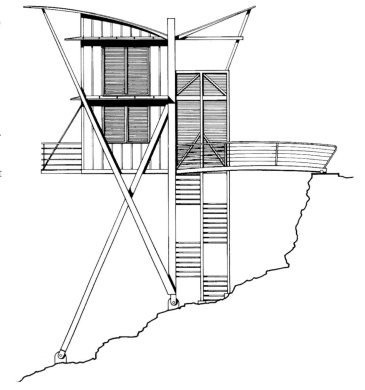

MICHAEL REYNOLDS

Earthships, Bolivia, Australia, Mexico, Scotland, Japan, Canada, Honduras, and USA, 1970s–present

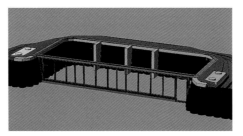

TOP DRAWING SHOWING THE PLANS FOR A U-SHAPED *EARTHSHIP*. THE TIRE WALL ACTS AS A BATTERY TO REGULATE THE HOME'S INTERIOR TEMPERATURE YEAR ROUND.

LEFT AN *EARTHSHIP* UNDER CONSTRUCTION IN FIFE, SCOTLAND. DISCARDED STEEL-BELTED TIRES ARE RAMMED WITH EARTH TO BECOME THREE-HUNDRED POUND BRICKS WHICH ARE STACKED ONE ON TOP OF THE OTHER TO FORM THE THREE-FOOT-THICK WALLS OF THE HOME.

OPPOSITE COMPLETED *EARTHSHIPS* IN THE UNITED STATES. EACH HOME IS SELF-SUSTANING AND NEEDS NEITHER A LOCAL UTILITY GRID OR FOSSIL FUEL FOR HEATING OR COOLING. PHOTOVOLTAIC CELLS CONNECTED TO EACH ROOF CONVERT SUNLIGHT INTO ELECTRICTY FOR DOMESTIC USE.

At Earthship Biotecture, garbage—in the form of tires and cans—is the essential building block of sustainable, off-grid private homes. With roots in the anti-establishment ideologies of the 1960s and 1970s, these self-built houses are increasingly the preferred dwellings of those weary or suspicious of being dependent on the utility systems ("grids") of existing cities.

For more than thirty years, Earthship founder and teacher, Michael Reynolds, has been touting the benefits of do-it-yourself, recycled housing. His *Earthships* are completely independent biospheres whose east, west, and north living areas recede into the ground and are wrapped by a wall of used, steel-belted auto tires rammed with earth. The three-foot-thick buttress acts like a battery, storing radiant and solar heat, which it releases at night and in winter to keep the interior at a constant temperature year-round without using fossil or nuclear fuels. Each *Earthship* provides its own electricity, via a photovoltaic power system mounted on its roof, as well as its own water, which is

collected from run-off, stored in cisterns, and filtered for use. All interior non-loadbearing walls are constructed of materials most people perceive as mere throwaways: aluminum cans and glass bottles.

However, beauty is in the eye and social consciousness of the beholder. True, the homes aren't available in colonial, ranch, or cape cod styles, but they do come in hut or "u" shapes, soft forms which may be integrated into the landscape rather than plopped down on it. Plus, the forms follow the function they are intended for: harnessing and conserving energy.

A pioneering desire to live in harmony with nature by disconnecting, literally, from a conventional, forced-air way of life is what brings all *Earthship* owners into fellowship with one another. In building and maintaining their own, unique homes, Earthshippers buy into and earn membership in a global community of like-minded believers who testify in an almost religious way to the merits of self-sufficiency.

Michael Reynolds, Earthship Biotecture, Taos, New Mexico, USA

SOFTROOM

Floating Retreat, concept for *wallpaper Magazine*, 1997
Tree House, concept for *wallpaper Magazine*, 1998

THIS PAGE INSPIRED IN PART BY THE AIRBAGS NASA EMPLOYED TO CUSHION PATHFINDER'S MARS LANDING, *FLOATING RETREAT* INFLATES TO PROVIDE SPECTACULAR VIEWS BOTH ABOVE AND BELOW THE SEA.

OPPOSITE THE *FLOATING RETREAT* MAY BE TOWED TO ANY LOCATION AND ANCHORED LIKE A BOAT. ONCE THE TOP IS OPENED, THE LID STABILIZES THE POD AND A GENERATOR INFLATES AN ENORMOUS POLYURETHANE DESERT ISLAND.

softroom, London, England

If we consider the role that nature plays in shaping today's domestic milieu, it is usually images of well-manicured lawns, flower beds, sprinklers, and swimming pools that spring to mind. Oliver Salway, Christopher Bagot, and Daniel Evans of London-based Softroom offer more radical ideas about how nature might intersect with culture.

Refusing to limit their work to purely practical applications, the firm produced a series of concepts for the design magazine *wallpaper*. *Tree House* was one such imaginative exercise in how architecture and nature might interact in relative harmony. With only the words "tree house" as a guide, the team developed a hypothetical, lightweight structure that blends into the trees. Attached to a large trunk with bolted collars, the *Tree House*'s ultra-minimal form suggests both a bird's nest and a hip temporary base at which to meet and eat before departing for other parts of the forest. When inhabitants aren't lounging on the deck or dining at a built-in picnic table, they may coast freely about the treetops in a sleeping cradle, which is winched along lengths of cable to adjacent trees. Lest anyone take their newfound animal freedom too literally, elastic webbing hangs below the home's perimeter to catch any false steppers.

Softroom's *Floating Retreat*, on the other hand (another concept for *wallpaper*), pushes nature into the realm of product. A tongue-in-cheek simulacrum of a real beach, the inflatable island is pure recreation. Both stowable and towable, the streamlined retreat resembles a blimp on wheels or a 1950s Airstream trailor. Once its top is popped, a generator inflates over a mile of polyurethane into any existing body of water, leaving the emptied hull to become a groovy floating beachhouse with all the accoutrements of the swinger: bedroom, bar, and living area with sound system and fiberglass sofas. Once the party is over, built-in firemen's hoses deflate the giant airbag so that it may be stuffed back into the pod for transport to a new location. Like its real-life *doppelgänger*, *Les Anthenea* (p. 60), *Floating Retreat* is yet another luxurious way for the active jetsetter to hang out for a few days *en plein air* without giving up civilization or compromising nature.

LEFT NATURE AND CULTURE COLLIDE IN NEW WAYS IN SOFTROOM'S *TREE HOUSE*. AFTER BEING HOISTED INTO POSITION, THE THREE, LIGHTWEIGHT FRAME SEGMENTS OF THE HOUSE'S DECK ARE SUPPORTED BY STRUCTURAL MEMBERS ATTACHED TO THE TRUNK VIA BOLTED COLLARS, CAUSING A MINIMUM OF DAMAGE TO THE BARK. HUNG FROM THE DECK ARE A CAPSULE CONTAINING THE WC AND A STORAGE UNIT THAT ACCEPTS THE DETACHABLE LUGGAGE FROM THE *FLOATING RETREAT*.

RIGHT THE *TREE HOUSE* IS REACHED BY A CLIMBING LADDER, THE LOWER SECTION OF WHICH, LIKE THAT ON A FIRE ESCAPE, CAN BE RETRACTED FOR SECURITY.

ARCHITECTUURSTUDIO HERMAN HERTZBERGER

watervilla, Middelburg, De Veersche Poort, The Netherlands, 1998–2002
semi-waterhouses, Ypenburg, The Netherlands, 1998 and ongoing

THIS PAGE IN THE NETHERLANDS, LAND IS CONTINUALLY RECLAIMED BY THE SEA. OUT OF NECESSITY, HERMAN HERTZBERGER HAS DESIGNED A PROTOTYPE *WATERVILLA* FOR THE MUNICIPALITY OF MIDDLEBURG. COMPACT, AND MORE OR LESS CYLINDRICAL IN SHAPE, THE HOME IS ACCESSED VIA A FOOTBRIDGE THAT KEEPS THE HOUSE FROM DRIFTING. WHEN DESIRED, THE HOUSE MAY BE TURNED ALMOST A FULL NINETY DEGREES, WITH THE HELP OF A WINCH, TO MAXIMIZE THE SUN'S ENERGY.

More than we may like to admit, nature is a force to be reckoned with when it comes to setting up house, especially in The Netherlands where land is forever being taken away by the sea. A typical response to this centuries-old tug-of-war with water has been the houseboat, a solution that is "too much boat and too little house" for Herman Hertzberger. In a radical reclamation of domestic space, he has plopped down a prototype, three-story, detached home directly into the port of Middelburg.

In a process related to the making of ships and yachts, the *watervilla* is constructed of a prefabricated steel skeleton with a low-maintenance metallic skin and steel-plate concrete floor. The lightweight structure rests on a triangular foundation of hollow, offshore, steel pipes, which enable it to drift at will without the rocking motion of a boat. In contrast to the Lilliputian quarters and appliances of other buoyant dwellings, the house has the scale and feel of a conventional one through the generous use of interior wood and amenities such as an atrium and roof terrace. Occupants may choose from several floor plans and exterior finishes, as well as decide on what kind of and how many rooms

are to be included. The main attraction of the home is that it capitalizes on water's fluid properties. Not only does water act as a cooling agent to help regulate the inside temperature, but it also enables the home to rotate almost a full ninety degrees. With the tug of a winch, or the push of a button, residents may move the home in whatever direction they please, towards the sun or away from it—a flexibility that results in substantial energy savings, greater privacy, and better views.

In Ypenburg, Hertzberger has gone even further in reclaiming inhabitable space from the water by extending the existing land. His eight *semi-waterhouses* rest on an artificial island of concrete in the form of a box, whose sunken bottom rests on the seabed to provide underground parking. The open "top" is filled with the houses themselves, whose diagonal living rooms provide spectacular views of the ocean.

In both scenarios, the houses are permanently connected to the shore and may be regarded as immovable property, facilitating the creation of a mortgage—a clever and heretofore underutilized method of colonizing water.

Architectuurstudio Herman Hertzberger, Amsterdam, The Netherlands

TOP THE COMPLEX IS DESIGNED LIKE A BOX, WHOSE BOTTOM RESTS ON THE SEABED TO PROVIDE UNDERWATER PARKING AND WHOSE TOP IS FILLED WITH THE HOUSES THEMSELVES.

BOTTOM IN A MANNER MIMICKING OFF-SHORE OIL RIGS, HERTZBERGER'S EIGHT *SEMI-WATERHOUSES* IN YPENBURG, THE NETHERLANDS, ARE CONNECTED TO LAND BY A CONCRETE PIER AND MAY BE ACCESSED BY FOOT OR CAR.

OOSTERHUIS. NL

variomatic House, **prototype dwelling, The Netherlands, 2000**

OPPOSITE A SELECTION OF THE MANY DIFFERENT EXTERIOR FORMS AND FACADES DEMONSTRATING THE ULTIMATE FLEXIBILITY OF *VARIOMATIC HOUSE*. THE CLADDING CAN BE ADJUSTED TO SUIT ANY ENVIRONMENT OR PERSONAL TASTE.

variomatic House is a concept for an adjustable dwelling, whereby the end user actively shapes his home. The exterior of this triangular building can be clad in an assortment of different patterned facades, enabling it to be hidden or conspicuous in any environment.

The unique design and manufacture of each *variomatic House* is made possible by machine-to-machine communication. until recently it was not possible to fabricate a building to unique specifications and make it as affordable as those produced on a mass scale. In the assembly of *variomatic House*, a direct line of communication is established between the three-dimensional modeling software it is designed with and the milling machine that fashions each component of the final construction.

Perhaps the most fascinating aspect of the *variomatic House* is the technology employed, not only in its design and construction but also in its operation. Kas oosterhuis intends for each *variomatic House* to learn about its inhabitants and their preferences in a manner similar to that of a personal computer memorizing the actions of its user. The house and inhabitant will grow more and more aware of each other and develop a personal relationship.

oosterhuis refers to his buildings as "bodies" because they are integrated into digital communication networks and can adapt and transform in response to the data they receive. *variomatic House*, like oosterhuis' other projects, can upgrade itself according to the wishes of its inhabitant or even as a reaction to climate change. This technology results in a constantly shifting or animated architecture and dispels with the notion that a building must have a static final image. "Architecture," as oosterhuis writes in the firm's mission statement, "is turning wild."

LACATON & VASSAL

***INDIVIDUAL HOUSE*, LÈGE CAP-FERRET, FRANCE, 1998**
***MINIMUM HOUSE*, ST. PARDOUX LA RIVIÈRE, FRANCE, 1998**

OPPOSITE THE FLOOR AND CEILING OF *INDIVIDUAL HOUSE* IS PERFORATED TO ALLOW THE TREES TO GROW STRAIGHT THROUGH. ALTHOUGH THE HOUSE HAS A METAL SHELL, IT IS BARELY NOTICEABLE AS IT RESTS AMONG THE TREES.

FOLLOWING PAGES *MINIMUM HOUSE* IS DRIVEN BY ECONOMIC LIMITATIONS AS IS EVIDENT IN THE WIDE APPLICATION OF INEXPENSIVE MATERIALS. THE RESULT IS A HUGE AREA OF DWELLING SPACE ON THE SMALLEST OF BUDGETS.

The inexpensive houses of Lacaton & Vassal are intended to have a limited life span, but this in no way compromises the quality of design. The materials and techniques they employ are industrial, yet their projects such as *Individual House* and *Minimum House* appear unobtrusive in their rural surroundings.

Lacaton & Vassal succeed in taking the ugliest materials, materials that have more in common with the temporary shelters on a construction site than the actual buildings under construction, and using them in such a way as to render them invisible. They achieve this by adopting an approach of non-architecture whereby any form of individual expression is completely ruled out.

Individual House, despite being made of galvanized steel and sheet aluminum, disappears into the trees it is built around. The trees pierce the house as if it had been dropped from a great height and impaled upon them. They are able to grow through the floor and ceiling of the house via a series of strategically placed holes skirted with flexible sleeves, which hug the tree trunks and move and grow as they do.

Minimum House is very matter of fact and a perfect example of Lacaton & Vassal's technique. The homeowner is an elderly lady who lives alone, but at weekends her grandchildren visit and her living space needs to accommodate them. The house resembles a barn or other simple agricultural shelters and so again recedes into its surroundings.

Lacaton & Vassal, Bordeaux, France

MONOLITHIC DOME INSTITUTE

Monolithic Domes, various locations, 1976 & ongoing
Cloud Hidden, Asheville, North Carolina, USA, 1998–2001

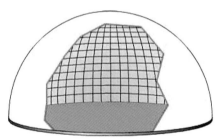

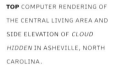

TOP COMPUTER RENDERING OF THE CENTRAL LIVING AREA AND SIDE ELEVATION OF *CLOUD HIDDEN* IN ASHEVILLE, NORTH CAROLINA.

If David B. South has his way, the world will convert and find itself happily at home in domes. As founder and president of the Monolithic Dome Institute, South envisions a future in which much of humanity will be encapsulated in global dome networks, the prototype of which he calls Domeville, U.S.A.

In fact, *Monolithic Domes* are so easy to construct and so basic in structure that he just might get his way. Anyone equipped with MD's patented Airform and instruction manual (first-timers can also take classes at the Institute) is ready to set up house with a handful of commonly manufactured building materials like concrete and rebar.

The method is simple: find a spot, lay a concrete foundation, inflate the fabric balloon, support with rebar, and spray concrete into place. One or more humps may be erected virtually anywhere and are seemingly at one with the landscape—in fact, many are also built underground—hugging the earth in a low-slung way that doesn't obscure the view or disturb the surrounding plant and animal life. But what endears homeowners most to the dome's primal form is how well it protects them from nature's forces, namely, tornadoes and hurricanes. In the Midwest and southern

united states, there is no safer place to be when annual twisters and tropical storms begin whipping through town. Because wind passes around the dome's rounded body, it can withstand gales of up to 150 mph and forces of up to 400 psf, thus serving as a sanctuary rather than an emergency shelter after the fact.

That is exactly why Jim and Melanie Kaslik erected the sleek *Cloud Hidden* in Asheville, North Carolina, where the elements routinely pose home maintenance problems. Resembling an alien craft, the house has large, curved openings which allow wind to surge through during a storm, preserving the home's living areas.

The big advantage of dome building is the chance to be one's own architect, so perhaps MD's promise of quality lifestyle and free expression may gel into an earthy, everyman's utopia. Since South introduced his system in 1976, *Monolithic Domes* have sprouted up in forty-five American states and many other countries because they are safe, energy efficient, and affordable alternatives to tract homes. Most importantly, for dwellers like the Kasliks, they represent a realizable way of thinking and living "outside the box."

IN JUST A FEW STEPS, DIYERS CAN BUILD A DOME THAT IS EASY ON THE ENVIRONMENT:
• LAY FOUNDATION
• INFLATE THE PATENTED AIRFORM
• SUPPORT WITH REBAR
• SPRAY WITH CONCRETE

OPPOSITE CARVED INTO A FORTY-FIVE DEGREE, SLOPED MOUNTAIN, JIM AND MELANIE KASLIK'S *CLOUD HIDDEN* SITS FIVE HUNDRED FEET ABOVE THE VALLEY. THE DOME IS A SIX-SEGMENT CATERPILLAR WHOSE THREE LEVELS HOUSE 5,300 SQUARE FEET OF LIVING SPACE. AS THE KALIKS POINT OUT, NO OTHER TYPE OF HOUSE WOULD GIVE THEM "THE INTERIOR SPACES, WIDE-OPEN ACCESS TO VIEWS, AND A FEELING OF SECURITY ON A RATHER PRECIPITOUS SITE."

FOLLOWING PAGES ARTIST'S RENDERING OF WHAT IT MIGHT LOOK LIKE IF THE COUNTRYSIDE WERE POPULATED BY COMMUNITIES OF DOME DWELLERS.

Monolithic Dome Institute, Italy, Texas, USA

RURAL STUDIO

corrugated construction, prototype dwelling, Auburn university, Newbern, Alabama, USA, 2001

It was under the instruction of samuel mockbee at Rural studio that the team of Gabriel comstock, Andrew olds, and Amy Jo Holtz designed and built *corrugated construction*. It is a prototype dwelling made from large bales of waste clippings that are created in the manufacturing process of corrugated cardboard. In order to produce boxes with a water-resistant finish, corrugated card is frequently given a special wax coating. This technique presents a problem because wax-coated card is very difficult to recycle. comstock, olds, and Holtz identified the tremendous potential of waxed corrugated bales as a useful construction material and developed a prototype house to analyze it further.

In their research, the trio found that one local factory alone was producing fifty waxed bales every day, each weighing around 1,000 pounds and heading straight to a landfill site. Although the bales are large, heavy, and need a forklift truck to lift them, they are relatively quick and easy to build with. The stacking of the walls in the prototype dwelling took only a day and a half to complete, but making it weatherproof required an additional protective coating. To achieve this the Rural studio students experimented with the use of vines and ivy as a living rain screen, however sheeting similar to that used in *9 stock orchard street* (p. 32) could also be used.

The corrugated building blocks are a contemporary remix of the traditional straw bale and replace hay with slithers of wax-coated card. The final texture resembles the tangled coat of a shaggy dog and this effect—when coupled with the fatness of the walls—provides a very effective means of insulation.

Different finishes including Portland cement and aluminum paint were applied to the bales to enable them to be used in other areas of the dwelling such as the foundations, the floor, and a door. Large timbers are used to frame the window and door openings and also provide a clean surface on top of the bale walls to which the roofing system is attached.

Rural studio was established by samuel mockbee at Auburn university in Alabama, U.S.A. It was here that he instigated an exemplary series of low-cost buildings to help house some of that region's poorest communities. Genuine innovations were made through his research into cheap, recycled materials and everyday technologies. Mockbee's influence is clear in the *corrugated construction* project—his former students have taken an inexpensive, widely available material and reworked it to create a valuable new addition to low-budget construction technologies.

samuel mockbee, gabriel comstock, andrew olds, and amy jo holtz – rural studio, newbern, alabama, usa

CHAPTER 3

BRING YOUR OWN BUILDING

set your life in motion by taking your home and even your office to whatever location you desire. today's nomads need never pack their bags. your house is your suitcase. no matter where you take your mobile dwelling unit, you'll always feel at home.

Most of the projects presented under the heading "Bring Your Own Building" acknowledge that the most attractive aspect of life on the move is not a sense of freedom, escape, and adventure but the special moments when isolated travelers converge to form a temporary community—the occasions when a fellow nomad is invited to bring his or her own building and gather round to form a new common space and social grouping.

It doesn't matter whether it's New Age travelers at an all-night rave or haulage drivers taking coffee at a truck stop, there is a tremendous sense of camaraderie among transient folk from all walks of life. This feeling is strengthened by the suspicious attitude mainstream society holds towards nomadic outsiders such as asylum seekers and traveling salespeople. Attitudes and phrases such as "trailer park trash" have certainly contributed to giving life on the road a bad reputation. It may be too late for the traveling salesman, but the ideas presented in this chapter attempt to improve the perception of transient living for individuals.

Office of Mobile Design's *Portable House* revisits the original objective of the mobile trailer home, which was to provide high-quality, affordable housing, often for those in a period of transition. The very term "trailer park" reeks of negative connotations, but this type of portable housing may well prove the ideal solution as western society becomes increasingly mobile. During a visit to a Florida trailer park, the journalist Chiori Santiago commented how "personalities literally spilled into the street...anonymity is impossible." Her observations highlight how privacy is abandoned to allow greater freedom for many of today's nomads. The potential ramifications of performing private activities in the public domain are explored in Valeska Peschke's *Instant Home* and Atelier van Lieshout's *Sportopia*, whereas the need for an intimate and private space while traveling through unfamiliar territory is explored in the PO.D's *Nomambule* and *Instant Ego*.

Several other projects featured here demonstrate ingenuity born out of poverty. Sean Godsell's *Future Shack*, Studio Orta's *Refuge Wear*, and Krzysztof Wodiczko's *Homeless vehicle* are all very different approaches to the basic human need for shelter, particularly in the extreme situations of war and natural disaster. Each aims to alleviate the suffering of refugees, the homeless, and other displaced people who have been forced to take to the road in order to stay alive.

A nomadic existence is not solely the preserve of the world's poor. For some it is simply a lifestyle choice. Alles wird Gut's *Turnon-urban sushi* units are intended to make life easier for the young, upwardly mobile urban dweller who skips from town to town and job to job. The super-wealthy have also long recognized the advantages of mobile living. The jet-setting millionaire avoids taxation and keeps a grip on his or her fortune by constantly moving from country to country. Offshore bank accounts and the global communications network enable this activity and governments seem powerless to prevent it.

The idea of a nomadic lifestyle conjures up many contrasting images encompassing everything from trail blazers to astronauts, hedonists at music festivals to their counterparts at caravan or RV conventions, the Bedouin to the Gypsy, wealthy tax exiles to poverty-stricken refugees, and the close-knit circus family to the loneliness of the long-distance trucker.

Mobility is a powerful weapon. Sam Peckinpah's movie *Convoy* (1978), inspired by the C. W. McCall song of the same name, demonstrates perfectly the inability of a static nation state to deal with a mobile community. In the movie, hundreds of truckers simply take to the road and form a massive convoy. The law enforcement authority's response to the truckers' provocation is to curtail their freedom and retaliate with violence. In many real cases governments simply ignore or outlaw the mobile way of life. N55 and Atelier van Lieshout demonstrate how mobility raises important issues concerning personal freedom in western democracies and how moving en mass presents real problems for those in charge.

ATELIER VAN LIESHOUT

compostopia, no fixed address, 2002
sportopia, no fixed address, 2002
AVL-ville, Rotterdam, The Netherlands, 2001
La Bais-ô-Drôme, no fixed address, 1995

All of Atelier van Lieshout's buildings are free of foundations. Mobility is a powerful weapon in AVL's explosive arsenal of wily provocations aimed at the state. Governments often seem threatened by nomads who live on the fringes of society, and AVL are no exception. Joep van Lieshout, AVL's founder, and his collaborators, manufacture portable buildings to question state control of civic facilities, such as the provision of water and sanitation.

Atelier van Lieshout create real working alternatives to the services usually provided by governments. In the project *AVL-ville*, a mini-state established in the port of Rotterdam, the group challenged the Dutch authorities to plan less and allow settlements to develop by themselves. *AVL-ville* was a victim of its own success and was forced to close in November 2001. All the elements of *AVL-ville* were mobile, including a farm, so the group were simply able to pack it all away and deliver the message elsewhere.

The majority of AVL's buildings are designed from the inside-out, a method which results in unusual projections and bulges in the exterior of each construction. Often the bed provides the starting point, as is seen in *La Bais-ô-Drôme*, a mobile home dedicated to "loving." At its core is a voluptuous bed littered

with ultra-soft pillows and beside it a minibar stocked with mood-enhancing drink. In a similar project *commune bed* (1998), AVL produced a bed large enough to hold a full scale orgy. Lining the sides of this bed were holsters carrying a selection of pornographic magazines, an assortment of sex toys, plus an array of drink and drugs to help cajole things along.

compostopia features a large bed with the capacity to sleep at least ten people, but here the bed looks very utilitarian and implies rest rather than recreation. As well as providing sleeping quarters, the *compostopia* construction comprises a small vegetable patch, a makeshift gym, washing facilities, and a compost toilet, the produce of which can be used to feed the garden. In *sportopia*, a variation of this assemblage, a cage was added for the practice of sadomasochistic sex. Here the effluent from the toilet can be recycled by channeling it into the cage to satisfy any visiting coprophiliacs. The basic structure is made from scaffolding poles allowing it to be easily erected at any location and in many different combinations.

sportopia embodies one of AVL's most prominent themes of the good, the bad, and the ugly: good in that it is self-sufficient and

promotes exercise; bad in that it can be used to perform dangerous sexual acts; and ugly in that it is made with scaffolding poles. This unification of the good, bad and ugly in AVL's work is a rejection of utopian ideals, a stance confirmed by Joep van Lieshout: "I don't believe in utopianism. I'm only interested in things I can realize. Utopian ideals rule out violence and crime and that's not realistic."

Atelier van Lieshout (AVL), Rotterdam, The Netherlands

Atelier van Lieshout (AVL), Rotterdam, The Netherlands

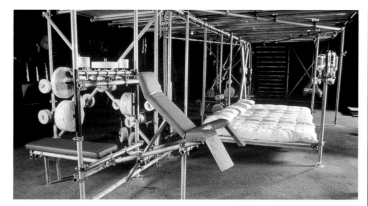

SEAN GODSELL ARCHITECTS
Future shack, no fixed address, 2001

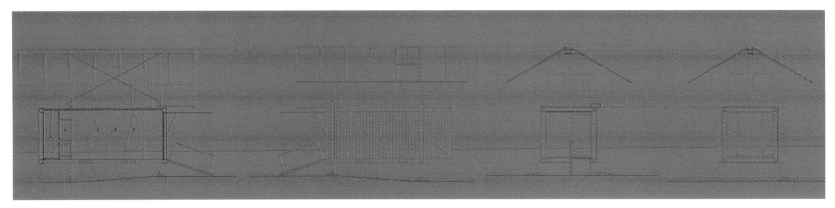

OPPOSITE TELESCOPIC LEGS, WHICH ARE PACKED INSIDE THE CONTAINER DURING TRANSIT, PROVIDE SUPPORT AND RULE OUT THE NEED FOR EXTENSIVE SITE PREPARATION.

TOP LEFT TO RIGHT CROSS SECTION SHOWING 1) CUPBOARD, 2) KITCHEN, 3) FOLDOUT BEDS, AND 4) LIVING/SLEEPING SPACE. SIDE ELEVATION, FRONT ELEVATION, AND BACK ELEVATION.

FOLLOWING PAGES INTERIOR VIEWS SHOWING THE BATHROOM FACILITIES AND THE FOLD-OUT BEDS, WHICH CAN BE STORED AWAY TO OPEN UP THE LIVING SPACE.

Future shack is a fold-away box of surprises intended to act as relief housing for refugees or victims of large-scale disasters. It is a fully portable, self-contained parcel complete with water tank, solar power cell, thermal insulation, air ventilation, and, because it is based on the universal specifications of the shipping crate, has a ready-made infrastructure with which to transport it.

The inclusion of a parasol roof sets *Future shack* apart from all other freight container dwellings. The prime mechanical function of the parasol is to deflect heat, but Godsell points to its other, equally important role when he describes its shape as a "universal symbol of home." The parasol roof softens the industrial edge of the container beneath, while also serving to make the unit much more homey.

The position and expanse of the roof create a domestic space beyond the confines of the shipping crate, and this openness makes it feel inviting.

The aura of domesticity is further enhanced by the fabric of the roof panels, which can be interchanged with indigenous materials such as thatch or palm to give *Future shack* an identity more in keeping with its location. The addition of telescopic legs rules out the need to prepare a foundation and means the unit can be situated in many different terrains.

The name *Future shack* is a play on the title of Alvin Toffler's 1970 book *Future shock*. In this social study, Toffler tells of the demise of the industrial era, and *Future shack* consolidates that demise by domesticating a familiar symbol of heavy industry.

sean godsell Architects, south yarra, victoria, Australia

sean godsell architects, south yarra, victoria, australia

VALESKA PESCHKE

Instant Home, california, usa, and berlin and dresden, germany, 1999 & ongoing

THIS PAGE THE *INSTANT HOME* TRAVELS IN A SIMPLE MOVING BOX AND TAKES ONLY TWO MINUTES TO INFLATE INTO A PITCHED-ROOF HOUSE COMPLETE WITH FURNITURE.

OPPOSITE PESCHKE HAS SET UP *INSTANT HOME* IN LOCATIONS TYPICALLY CONSIDERED UNINHABITABLE, FROM CITY PARKING LOTS, TO SUBURBAN DRIVEWAYS, TO THE DESERTS OF THE WESTERN UNITED STATES.

as any homeless person of today knows, lurking about someone else's property offers immediate lessons on the difference between belonging to the group and being on the outside, personal freedom and public vagrancy, private rights and trespassing on private property. yet as berlin-based artist valeska peschke demonstrates with her transportable *Instant Home*, squatting and loitering may also be manipulated to merge private desires with public space.

without a permanent home of her own, peschke has been traversing the u.s. and europe in a pick-up truck, setting up "house" whenever and wherever the urge seizes her. rather than put up a tent, however, peschke inflates a 150-square-foot vinyl parody of the conventional, landlocked suburban dream with all its amenities. ready to use in two minutes, her *Instant Home* contains all the comforts of a middle-class bungalow: a sofa, lamp, coffee table, fireplace, and television— all of which are blown up, literally, into soft, squishy caricatures of their former selves. And while overstuffed furniture has typically been a signifier of adult, middle-class taste, here the stereotype is exaggerated to a childlike extreme.

That the home resembles a child's playhouse is perhaps why peschke has been allowed to linger longer in the otherwise off-limit spaces where she has dropped anchor, from the driveways of suburban residences to the parking lots of downtown office districts. Her house is a nonaggressive, fun place to "hang out," a valued activity in western cultures where frenetic mobility is tempered by an emphasis on leisure time.

even so, public ordinances do not necessarily keep pace with changes in contemporary lifestyle, which is where peschke's project upsets the delicate balance between infinite freedom of movement and social decline, hanging out and dropping out. In this respect, her project shares affinities with that of activists in berlin who squatted empty buildings throughout the late 1970s and early 1980s in protest of the city's lack of adequate housing.

Likewise, peschke approaches the idea of domestic space from the perspective of intervention to open up some very fundamental socioeconomic and architectural issues. what constitutes a house? what form should it take? And, most importantly, why should it be "private"?

valeska peschke, lives and works in berlin, germany

valeska peschke, lives and works in Berlin, Germany

JENNIFER SIEGAL, OFFICE OF MOBILE DESIGN

Portable House, no fixed address, 2001

OPPOSITE A SERIES OF
EXPANDABLE/CONTRACTIBLE
SPACES RENDER THE *PORTABLE
HOUSE* COMPLETELY FLEXIBLE
AND ADAPTABLE. WHETHER
BRIEFLY SITUATED IN AN URBAN
SPACE, OR POSITIONED FOR A
MORE LENGTHY STAY IN THE
OPEN COUNTRY, THE *PORTABLE
HOUSE* HAS A MINIMUM IMPACT
ON ITS LOCATION.

TOP OMD CHALLENGE
PRECONCEIVED IDEAS ABOUT
THE TRAILER HOME AND THE
TRAILER PARK BY CREATING AN
AFFORDABLE OPTION FOR
THOSE LACKING THE RESOURCES
TO ENTER THE CONVENTIONAL
HOUSING MARKET.

office of Mobile Design's *Portable House* is born of the same californian culture that gave rise to gaudy hot dog stands and the enigma of the western gunslinger. Jennifer Siegal, the founder of OMD, is based in Los Angeles, a city where buildings are just temporary fixtures. the architecture of the earthquake-prone city reflects a completely different mentality to that which spawned the grand boulevards of Paris and other older cities. A drive across the grid-pattern streets of L.A. reveals a city of boxes. the decoration of these buildings may change, but the basic structure is essentially a disposable, square container. Empty lots come and go in rapid succession, leaving piles of rubble between periods of demolition and construction. OMD is rethinking and re-establishing methods of building to provide an antidote to what they describe as the "generic clutter," which increasingly obstructs the L.A. landscape.

siegal's grandfather had a business selling hot dogs from a portable kiosk and while studying architecture, she did too. siegal admits the portable hot dog stand has made a lasting impression on her thinking and this is evident in her mobile architecture. *Portable House* is based on the same structural system as a typical portable classroom and is conceived as an affordable option for those living a transient lifestyle. the concept challenges the stigma commonly associated with trailer park housing and adapts to or creates new social dynamics wherever it is placed. gathered together, a group of units are able to establish a common space effectively forming a courtyard or garden for social interaction.

Portable House recalls an era of the old west when the covered wagon could be transformed to accommodate a variety of functions and conditions. similarly, the OMD dwelling unit is rendered completely flexible by its expandable/contractible spaces and its all around mobility. *Portable House* revisits the romantic western idea of a life spent drifting from town to town. it responds to the needs of a generation that has traded in the six-shooter for a cellular phone and a laptop.

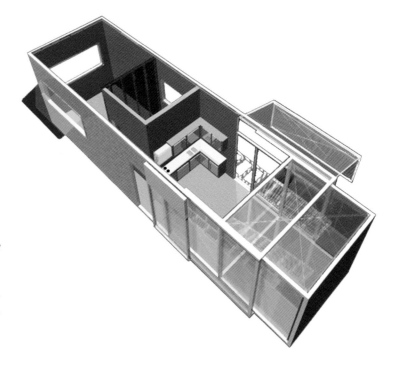

PO.D

INSTANT EGO, prototype dwelling by Hyoungjin cho, Rémi Feghali, and Adrien Raoul, Paris, 2000

NOMAMBULE, prototype dwelling by Lotfi sidirahal and whookiat Heng, Paris, 1999

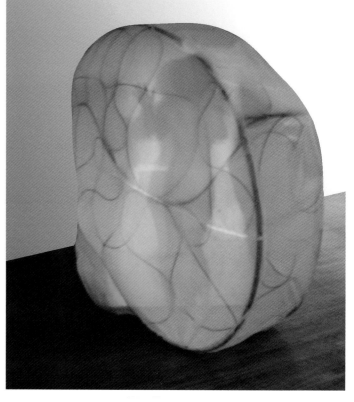

TOP LEFT A SERIES OF ELECTRONIC SENSORS LOCATED IN THE COCKPIT OF INSTANT EGO ENABLE THE SEATED PILOT TO STEER A PATH THROUGH A PROJECTED CYBER SPACE LANDSCAPE.

TOP RIGHT THE OVERALL FORM OF INSTANT EGO IS GENERATED FROM THE RELATIONSHIP BETWEEN THE BODY AND SPACE.

BOTTOM INSTANT EGO IS ENCAPSULATED WITHIN AN INFLATED MEMBRANE, THE PATTERN OF WHICH RESEMBLES A CHRYSALIS OR THE GOSSAMER WINGS OF A DRAGONFLY.

with INSTANT EGO and NOMAMBULE, PO.D have created architecture-on-demand: buildings that are there when you want and packed away when you don't. the two proposals give instant gratification and bring architecture into line with services such as pay-per-view television or pay-as-you-talk mobile telephones.

INSTANT EGO is in many ways a similar project to NOMAMBULE but once the user has entered the inner chamber of this device, he or she is plunged into the unknown and infinite realm of cyber space. the dwelling attempts to answer how it feels to travel inside your own pocket. it starts out like a foldaway hood on a raincoat: you unzip the contraption from your jacket pocket and it expands to eventually swallow you whole. However, once you have disappeared inside INSTANT EGO, its confined space is made infinite via the endless realm of virtual reality, which is projected onto its inner skin. you can then travel into this infinite space while remaining seated by a series of electronic sensors that manipulate the projected image to follow your movements.

NOMAMBULE is a take-anywhere inflatable structure that performs a function not dissimilar to that of the sony walkman. the sony walkman provides its user with an anchor to a familiar experience when the listener plays

back their own choice of music while passing through an unknown location. what the sony walkman channels aurally the NOMAMBULE gives spatially and at a moment's notice can be pumped up to form a familiar personal space for its user. PO.D describe NOMAMBULE as an "affectionate container of the self," and liken its purpose to a child's teddy bear or security blanket. NOMAMBULE is a protective bubble intended to make its user feel at home wherever he or she might be. it was conceived in response to the specific need for an intimate and familiar space when traveling to new and unusual locations. A ring of inflated pillows forms an inner chamber, inside which the user is able to relax in an air-cushioned realm of familiar space.

INSTANT EGO and NOMAMBULE are both inflatable accessories to facilitate a nomadic lifestyle. PO.D identified that, in general, people spend a significant amount of their time on the move and consequently many hours are spent in limbo, for example waiting for a train to arrive or a plane to take off. INSTANT EGO and NOMAMBULE, were conceived to fill these moments of lost time. Both structures are extensions of the body and materialize from a backpack or pocket to provide an intimate space where once there was none.

PO.D, Paris, France

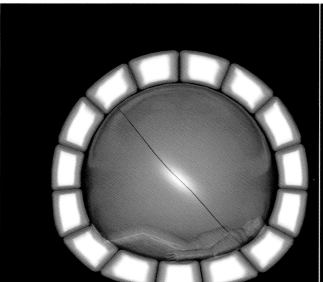

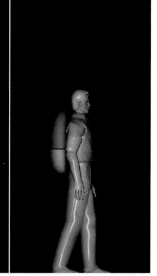

TOP RIGHT PO.D ARE HEAVILY
INFLUENCED BY RADICAL
ARCHITECTURAL COLLECTIVES
OF THE 1960S, SUCH AS HAUS-
RUCKER-CO. AND ARCHIGRAM.
SEE ARCHIGRAM'S *CUSHICLE*
ON PAGE 11.

LEFT THESE COMPUTER-
RENDERED DRAWINGS
DEMONSTRATE HOW THE
NOMAMBULE CAN BE CARRIED
IN A BACK PACK AND INFLATED
ON DEMAND BY A CYLINDER OF
COMPRESSED AIR.

LUCY ORTA, STUDIO ORTA

Refuge wear, no fixed address, 1992 & ongoing
Modular Architecture, no fixed address, 1996 & ongoing

Studio Orta demolish the boundary between architecture and fashion. Their nomadic creations can be defined as both "buildings to wear" and "clothes to live in," underlining the belief of Lucy Orta, the studio's founder, that "clothes are fully entitled to become architectural dwellings."

Refuge wear is similar to Krzysztof Wodiczko's *Homeless vehicle* (p. 118) in that it provides a survival system for people of no fixed address. *Refuge wear* began in 1992 as a series of drawings in response to human catastrophes that caused the displacement of whole populations. These sketches were fabricated into a collection of bodysuits, which rapidly transform into tent-like shelters by a system of zip and velcro fasteners. The realized articles represent the idea of architecture as an extension of the body and resemble the bodysuits designed to protect against chemical weapons in the theater of war. The pac-a-mac technology employed in *Refuge wear* later provided life-saving mobile accommodation in situations as diverse as the Kurdish refugee crisis, the horrific war in Rwanda, and homelessness on the streets of Paris.

Modular Architecture updates the system used in *Refuge wear*, which essentially caters to the individual, to accommodate collective activity. The system devised for *Modular Architecture* allows for its users to travel freely as individuals, but should a group of two or more nomads converge on a single location, they can zip their bodysuits together to create a warm and spacious temporary house.

Solidarity and collective action are major themes of Studio Orta's output. The early project *Refuge wear* functions as a survival tool in extreme conditions, but the person wearing the outfit remains isolated from fellow users. *Modular Architecture* bridges this important gap by building physical connections between displaced people. This link recognizes that social bonds and shared experience are almost as essential to surviving in extreme situations as food, water, and medicine.

Lucy Orta, Studio Orta, Paris, France

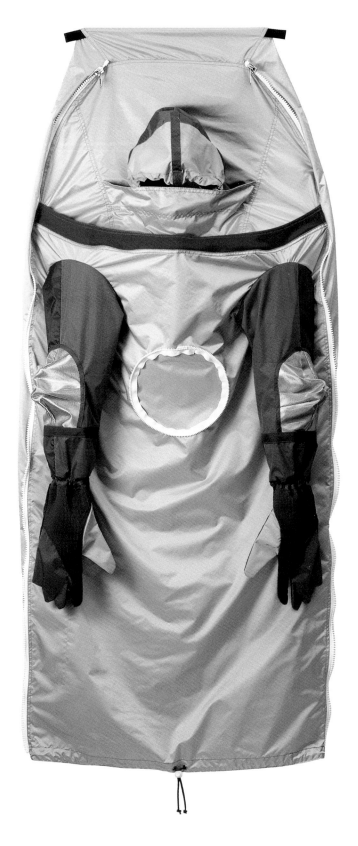

Lucy orta, studio orta, paris, france

NADER KHALILI, CAL-EARTH

superadobe domes, USA, Iran, Iraq, 1991 & ongoing

TOP AND OPPOSITE STUTTGART NATIVE GERWIG ROTH, WHO STUDIED UNDER NADER KHALILI IN CALIFORNIA, BUILT THE DOMES ON THESE PAGES USING THE *SUPERADOBE* TECHNIQUE. EACH DOME IS MADE OF LONG TUBES OF MATERIAL FILLED WITH EARTH, WHICH ARE HELD TOGETHER WITH BARBED WIRE. SIMPLE WOODEN FORMS WERE EMPLOYED TO GIVE EACH OPENING A UNIQUE SHAPE.

Given the choice between erecting a skyscraper and scraping in the soil, Nader Khalili would gladly accept a day in the dirt. It takes a lot of digging to construct his *superadobe* shelters, which consist of sausage-skin-like coils of earth-filled sandbags held together with barbed wire.

Originally a designer of corporate high rises, Iranian-born Khalili sold his practices in Tehran and Los Angeles in 1975 to embark on a motorcycle tour of rural Persia that would last five years. what he rediscovered on that homeward trek has already led to innovative and safe temporary housing for the world's one billion homeless and may soon determine whether, and how, humans might live on the moon.

In Iran Khalili again encountered the age-old method of mud-brick building, which he updated and simplified for what he foresaw as its broader global applications: refugee, emergency, and relief housing. Back in the U.S., Khalili transformed elements of war and containment—sandbags and wire—into places of refuge and peace. capable of withstanding earthquakes, the domes are cost-effective alternatives to shanties cobbled together from plywood, tin, or plastic sheets. Plus, the bags can be dropped at or carried to any location,

making the technique quickly adaptable to populations on the move. slowly but surely governments are getting the picture. Following the Iran-Iraq war, for example, forty *superadobes* were constructed in Iran, and there is talk of the concept being implemented in Afghanistan.

The concept is so fundamental and flexible that even NASA has considered ways it could be used to populate the moon. The bags would stay the same but would be filled with moon dust and held in place with velcro instead of barbed wire. so far it hasn't happened, but in the meantime Khalili isn't wasting any time. This year he obtained permission to construct a model lunar colony in Hesperia, fifty miles north of Los Angeles.

Being a modular system, the potential exists for *superadobes* to multiply across the planet, forming neighborhoods, even cities. And this is no coincidence. Like other visionaries before him, from Le Corbusier to Levitt, Khalili sees a bigger picture in which whole communities of his ecological, organic domes will spring up—which explains the construction of a coiled, three-bedroom, two-car garage compound alongside the lunar prototypes.

Nader Khalili, Cal-Earth (California Institute of Earth Art & Architecture), Hesperia, California, USA

KRZYSZTOF WODICZKO

Homeless vehicle project, NEW YORK and BOSTON, USA, 1988 & ongoing

TOP THE METAL NOSE CONE OPERATES AS AN EMERGENCY EXIT, A CONTAINER FOR THE WASH BASIN AND TOOLS AND, WHEN OPENED, CAN BE USED AS A SINK FOR WASHING OR AS A BARBECUE FOR COOKING.

A: "WHAT I'M SAYING IS THOSE SNOW CONE CARTS USE GLASS ON TOP, AND FOR YOU, FOR YOUR SAFETY, FOR YOU TO SLEEP..."
K: "YOU'RE SAYING ITS BETTER IF YOU'RE VISIBLE, SO PEOPLE KNOW YOU ARE THERE, RATHER THAN HIDDEN?"
A: "YES. WHAT ABOUT IF SOMEONE GETS MAD OR SOMETHING? AT LEAST THEY COULD SEE THAT SOMEBODY'S IN THERE."

An affordable, architect-designed live/work space in the center of NEW YORK is likely to be an attractive proposition for any upwardly mobile professional seeking accommodation in that crowded city. This was certainly the case for Alvin, "A," Oscar, and Victor, four members of NEW YORK's homeless scavenging community.

Krzysztof Wodiczko conceived the *Homeless vehicle project* in response to the specific needs of this small congregation of homeless individuals, who all live outside NEW YORK's dormitory shelter program. The four individuals earn money as bottle men. They walk the streets collecting recyclable bottles and cans in return for a small cash deposit. In a city where uniformed officers are deployed to keep the public parks and plazas free of homeless people, mobility has become an essential survival tactic for the scavenging community.

A need was identified to design a vehicle

that might help Alvin, "A," Oscar, and Victor to travel easily from one place to another, while also providing a place to sleep and carry securely their personal belongings and their haul of bottles and cans. Wodiczko developed a prototype version of the vehicle in collaboration with the four bottle men. In a series of discussions, the group determined that their new live/work space be safely and easily maneuverable, include sleeping, washing, and cooking facilities, and have plenty of storage space for the collected bottles and cans. The prototype was then tested on the streets by the four men and modifications were made in accordance with each of their suggestions.

Wodiczko believes firmly that this collaborative process is essential to the project's success. He states, "only through such cooperation can the vehicle function usefully. Direct participation of users in the

construction of the vehicle is the key to developing a vehicle that belongs to its users, rather than merely being appropriated by them."

The working vehicles resemble street vendor's carts or street cleaner's trolleys, and therefore conform to the utilitarian nature of other portable structures seen on the sidewalks of NEW YORK. Moreover, by making the activities of the bottle men visible, the *Homeless vehicle* takes an active part in altering the public's perception of homeless individuals. Alvin, "A," Oscar, and Victor, and others since, can no longer be ignored or walked away from. The nomadic bottle men stake a legitimate claim to their citizenship of NEW YORK CITY by performing a useful function within that society.

Krzysztof Wodiczko, lives and works in BOSTON, Massachusetts, USA

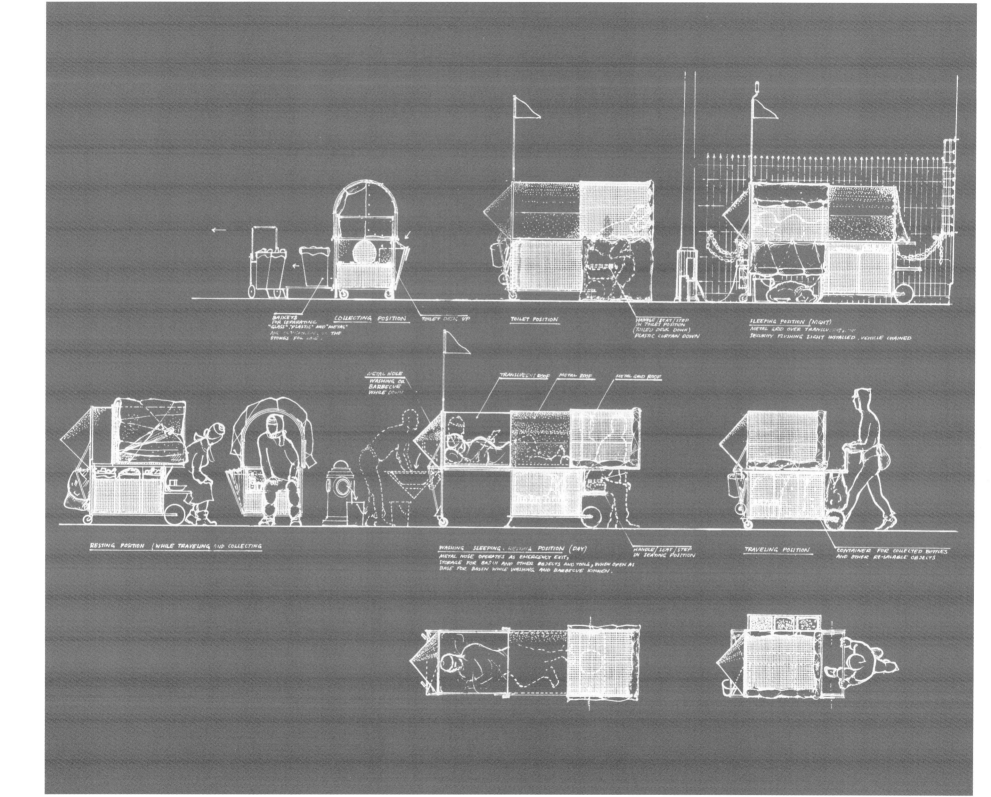

ANDREA ZITTEL

A–z Living unit, 1994
A–z escape vehicles, 1996
A–z cellular compartment units, 2001

THIS PAGE PORTABLE AND ECONOMICAL, EACH *A–Z LIVING UNIT* IS MODELED ON A STEAMER TRUNK AND, WHEN UNFOLDED, IS MEANT TO FUNCTION AND BE USEFUL IN EVERYDAY LIFE, AS OPPOSED TO BEING A MERE DESIGN OBJECT. "EVEN THOUGH OUR LIVES ARE INCREASINGLY TRANSIENT," AS AZAS STATES, "THE NEED FOR A SENSE OF HOME REMAINS AND OUR REQUIREMENTS FOR PROTECTION, COMFORT, AND INDIVIDUALITY ENDURE."

OPPOSITE TWO VERSIONS OF ZITTEL'S *A–Z ESCAPE VEHICLES,* A CONTEMPORARY WAY TO FIND REFUGE. ONE CLIENT TURNED THE VEHICLE INTO A PRINCESS-LIKE LOUNGE, WHILE ANOTHER PREFERRED A MORE SCHOLARLY RETREAT.

operating in the gap between art and architecture, Andrea Zittel creates inhabitable sculptures and installations which she advertises and sells through a mock company, A–Z Administrative Services. In a parody of the automotive industry, Administrative Services routinely releases new lines of furniture, homes, and vehicles for today's transient consumer. While many of AZAS's products are innovative examples of transportable domestic architecture, it is not necessarily freedom of movement that informs their design. Rather, their cozy forms cater to consumers seeking security and the illusion of home when on the move. Even so, AZAS simply provides the form. You must supply the content.

End-user input is essential to the proper functioning of the *A–z cellular compartment units.* Each home is a network of chamber-like boxes which may be stacked or moved around like toy blocks. The down-to-earth cubicles resemble their plastic versions in playgrounds the world over and have rounded crawlspaces which lead occupants through multiple carpeted compartments and daily tasks, from sleeping and eating to working and working out. But again, AZAS merely builds the shells. How basic or decadent they are entirely depends on the personality of the owner.

Similarly *A–z escape vehicles* are factory-built, recreational enclosures waiting for a personal touch. Currently customized examples include a Joseph Cornellesque study with writing desk and a Cinderella-like carriage with wet bar. The possibilities are endless and no matter what the owner chooses to do inside, absolute privacy is ensured by a locking hatch. Like the trailer park homes on which they are based, the capsules may be hauled to new locations and parked for long periods, but fundamentally they are about a secret inner world "[where you] won't have to answer to anybody else's laws, rules, standards, or expectations."

The somewhat earlier *A–z Living units* offer a more conventional take on personal liberty. Modeled on a steamer trunk, each unit unfolds into a forty-four-square-foot module equipped with necessities such as a kitchen, bedroom, or vanity. To counteract the somewhat impersonal side of its industrial manufacture, each mini flat must be retrofitted, modified, and imbued with gesture and content by its occupant. The result is an instant home authored as much by the end user as the designer.

With over ten product lines to choose from, there is a format and function to suit any taste.

The most difficult part of living on the loose is deciding on what model, make, and accessories suit your needs. But by logging onto AZAS's web site and perusing the possibilities, the convenience and purchase of a personally defined universe is just a mouse click away.

Andrea Zittel, A–z Administrative Services, Brooklyn, New York, and Joshua Tree, California, USA

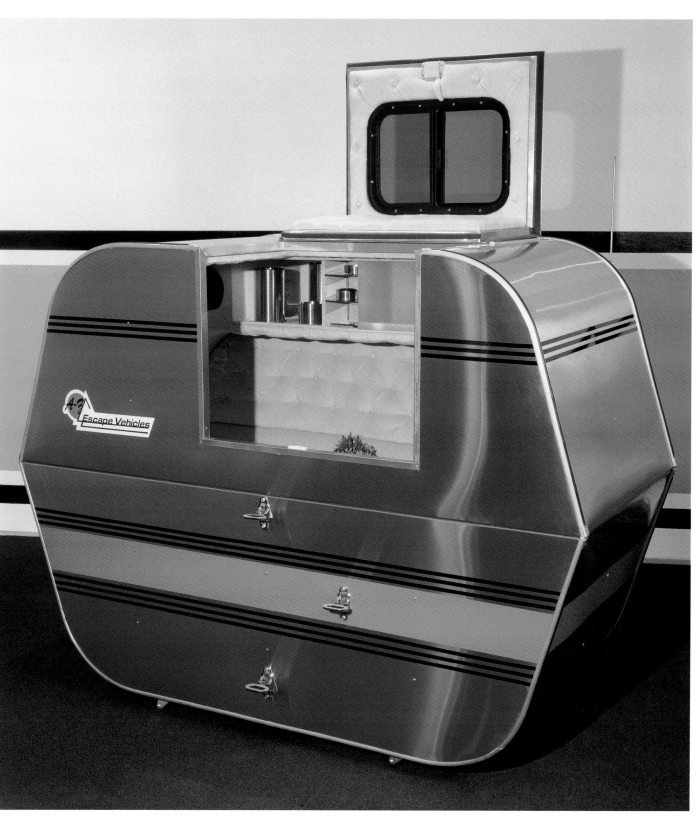

Andrea Zittel, A–Z Administrative Services, Brooklyn, New York, and Joshua Tree, California, USA

OPPOSITE AND LEFT ZITTEL'S
*A–Z CELLULAR COMPARTMENT
UNITS* ALLOW EVERY NEED,
TASK, OR DESIRE TO HAVE ITS
OWN SPACE AND TIME.
INDIVIDUAL BOXES MAY BE
CUSTOMIZED AND LINKED
TOGETHER TO FORM A HIGHLY
PERSONAL COMPOUND.

TOP RIGHT IN DEVELOPING
THE UNITS, ZITTEL TRIED TO
IMAGINE WHAT IT WOULD FEEL
LIKE TO FUNCTION IN SMALL,
STACKING ROOMS. MOVING
THROUGH A SERIES OF THESE
SPACES IS SIMILAR TO WHAT
PETS MUST EXPERIENCE IN
THE TUNNELS AND NESTS OF
HABITRAILS.

AWG_ALLES WIRD GUT

turnon – urban sushi, 2000

RIGHT SILHOUETTES OF *TURN-ONS* IN ALL THEIR DIFFERENT COMBINATIONS.

OPPOSITE "A SERIES OF REVOLVING MODULES—LIKE GIANT HAMSTER WHEELS—CONTAIN ALL LIVING PROGRAMS. THERE IS NO DISTINCTION ANYMORE BETWEEN WALL, FLOOR, OR CEILING—JUST ONE TRANSITIONAL SPACE, ALL IN ONE, ALL AT THE SAME TIME. WHILE COOKING, THE COUCH BECOMES THE CEILING, THE DINING TABLE A WALL...THE INTERIOR SPACE CHANGES CONSTANTLY WITH THE ENDLESS POSITIONS OF EACH RING—A NEW FLAT EVERY DAY."—ALLES WIRD GUT

LIFE is a series of circular motions, so why not go with the flow when it comes to housing? THE advantages of spinning 360 degrees are many, which is why AWG_ALLES WIRD GUT, a five-member design collaborative working in vienna, propose that we all live in wheels.

THE concept behind their *turnon-urban sushi* unit is that multiple living functions can be compressed into a ten-foot-high wheel and accessed at will by simply rolling in place. AS evidenced by the prototype, which rests on a steel frame and floats on magnetic rails, a quick push will take residents from the couch in one arc to a table and two chairs in another to a chaise longue in a third. Every surface can be lived in and on. when different modules are joined together, the result is a giant tube of endless lifestyle possibilities.

what has informed awg's design more than anything else is the automobile industry, where advances in prefabrication, mass-production, and accessorizing have reached a level of sophistication unequaled in the engineering of housing. AS the European smart™ car has demonstrated, autos may be quickly and infinitely upgraded or changed with clip-on parts in distinctive colors to suit any taste. Likewise, *turnons* are available in a wide variety of materials (metal, wood,

awg_Alles wird gut, vienna, Austria

fiberglass, or rubber), functions, and styles to mix and match, as evidenced by the "spice," "carefree," and "avant-garde" series. the most popular module at the moment is the "wet cell," which incorporates bathroom and kitchen into one rotation. all of the options are detailed in a catalogue which reads like a contemporary car ad: "restrictions vanish, dreams come true."

of course not many people live in their cars, so who would be willing to occupy a wheel? According to awg, the target customers are young urban singles who move around a lot and don't spend much time at home. Indeed, the wheel is an optimal way to increase the amount of living space in a cramped inner-city flat. After all, it was the need for small animals to have a change of scenery and to get enough exercise within confined quarters that led to the invention of the hamster wheel.

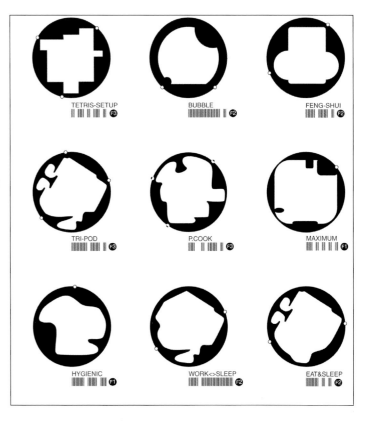

TETRIS-SETUP   BUBBLE   FENG-SHUI

TRI-POD   P.COOK   MAXIMUM

HYGIENIC   WORK<>SLEEP   EAT&SLEEP

ΛVΛNTGΛRDE

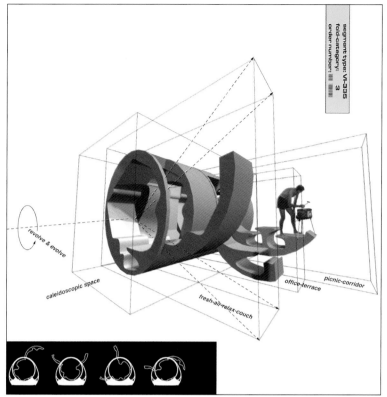

segment type: VI-335
fold-category: 3
order number:

revolve & evolve

caleidoscopic space

fresh-air-relax-couch

office-terrace

picnic-corridor

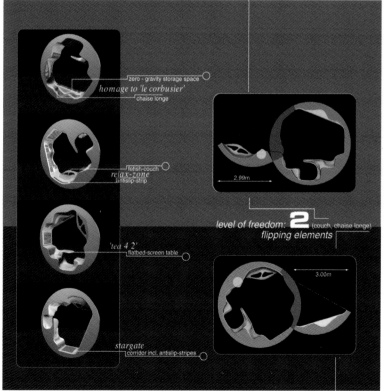

zero - gravity storage space

homage to 'le corbusier'
chaise longe

fetish-couch
relax-zone
antislip-strip

2.99m

'tea 4 2'
flatbed-screen table

level of freedom: **2** (couch, chaise longe)
flipping elements

3.00m

stargate
corridor incl. antislip-stripes

awg_Alles wird Gut, vienna, austria

N55

snail shell system, prototype vehicle,
no fixed address, 2000 & ongoing

OPPOSITE THE INTERIOR OF THE *SNAIL SHELL* IS LINED WITH FOAM FOR ADDED COMFORT AND INSULATION. THE LASHINGS ON THE EQUIPMENT BOX ENSURE THAT ALL THE TOOLS ARE HELD IN PLACE WHILE THE UNIT IS IN MOTION.

TOP RIGHT THE *SNAIL SHELL SYSTEM* IS DESIGNED TO BE TAKEN ANYWHERE, EVEN ON WATER OR UNDERGROUND.

BOTTOM RIGHT TWO RUBBER CATERPILLAR TRACKS AID MANEUVERABILITY WHEN THE *SNAIL SHELL* IS ROLLED FROM PLACE TO PLACE.

snail shell system is a roll around, inhabitable container constructed from an inexpensive, polyethylene cylinder. It enables its user to change his whereabouts and live in different environments, including on water and underground. The compact system measures just over thirty nine inches in height and sixty inches in diameter and takes up very little space wherever it is placed. The material used is non-toxic, low in weight, and sturdy to allow for the unit to be partly buried where the ground permits or to be floated on water. *snail shell system* can also be used as a comfortable space or extra room inside an existing building.

The technology behind the device is clever yet practical. Every component has at least two functions in order to maximize the limited space. The cylindrical container can be rolled easily from place to place. Maneuverability is further enhanced by two detachable caterpillar tracks that are made from rubber doormats and protect the shell of the container from damage while in motion. The unit also floats on water, and in this situation the caterpillar tracks function as protective fenders when it is moored. To move the vessel on water one can either row it with a paddle, use a kite to act like a sail, or hook it up to a motorboat for towing.

snail shell system comes complete with its own equipment box, which contains a bilge pump that doubles up as a vacuum cleaner and a shower, hoses for the pump, kitchen pan, kettle, and alcohol burner, and foldable water containers that can be used for ballast as well as the shower. In addition to this, the equipment box itself can be emptied, lined with a plastic bag, and used as a toilet.

All kinds of extensions can be added to the vessel depending on the situation it is placed into. Dynamos or solar panels can be added so the *snail shell system* has its own power source. Links can also be attached to combine several units, but because polyethylene cannot be successfully glued to other materials, any add-ons must be connected by bolting or lashing.

N55 have developed a system combining the suitcase on wheels with the mobile home. It is a useful traveling companion and affordable motel in a single, attractive pod.

N55, copenhagen, Denmark

CHAPTER 4

SPACE INVADERS

why not breathe some life into dead urban and suburban spaces by inserting homes into unused gaps? Real estate is always at a premium so find a space and cling to it. Adapt to your neighbor's living space or make room for your own by latching onto theirs.

The homes in this chapter offer both playful and aggressive solutions to the ongoing problem of finding and keeping residential space in crowded cities. since the industrial revolution, the options have tended to polarize around making do with cramped, noisy, and often unsanitary flats in town or fleeing to the surrounding countryside for fresh air and room to roam. in the nineteenth century, this meant living in a tenement or commuting to a garden city; in the twentieth century, it was the choice between a high rise or the suburbs. with the onset of the twenty-first century, the preponderance of edge cities in the u.s. and elsewhere has demonstrated that in-between alternatives are greatly desired, if not yet ideal or satisfactory.

It used to be that the inner city was the unfortunate domain of the industrial worker who could not afford to escape to nature. Now that we inhabit a postindustrial landscape, urban hubs are cleaner, safer, and more attractive to the middle and upper classes, who deserted them for lawns and gardens. People are returning to the center in droves, pushing rents up and lower-income residents out, and increasing the need for in-town housing that fulfills the needs of people from varying socioeconomic brackets. The homes herein represent a yeasty cross section of what's currently on the market—or coming soon.

Architects, collectives, artists, and individuals have responded to the problem of less space for more money with highly functional city homes that range from the witty to the parasitic. In many instances, skills that children acquire early on—stacking and hanging objects, inserting blocks into slots, or blowing up balloons—have allowed homeowners and designers alike to approach spatial problems from the liberating perspective of play.

In Germany, for example, artist stefan eberstadt is experimenting with homes that hang by straps. His *rucksack houses* are intended to dangle gleefully from the chimneys of existing apartment buildings to provide extra living space for the students and guest workers who inhabit munich's numerous one-room studios. In Japan, coelacanth & associates have traded the blueprint for three-dimensional cubes, which they encourage their clients to rearrange into combinations that suit their needs. The final configurations become prefabricated homes, called *space blocks*, which make the most of the owner's personal fancy as well as the limitations of any snug site. Piercy conner architects' *microflat* proposal for london is an exercise in placing rectangles into the right-sized holes. Each *microflat* is an elongated box intended to house one working-class individual. when several units are stacked on top of one another, they may be inserted into unused urban gaps, from parking lots to rooftops, forming an instant, ad hoc community. Along the same lines, but on the upper end of the economic scale, is LOT/EK's *Guzman Penthouse*, a private home made of shipping containers which have been stacked on top of a factory loft in Manhattan.

In all of these cases, play is not to be equated with fooling around or shirking responsibility but with achieving personal independence. This is nowhere more apparent than in Michael Rakowitz's inflatable *parasITE* homeless shelters, which attach to the exhaust systems of public buildings. Their squishy membranes and funky shapes share affinities with beach toys; however, each pod is a private and interim alternative to living in a church basement or the YMCA.

The suburbs have not been immune to overcrowding either, particularly in Japan, where land is scarce. Ushida Findlay Architects have responded with their *Truss Wall House* whose free-flowing curves open up an otherwise rigid, square site. The situation is somewhat different in the United States, where tracts of inhabitable land—those islands of grass commonly known as front and back yards—are routinely wasted in the service of keeping the neighbors at bay. California-based Jones, Partners: Architecture is aggressively reclaiming the extra square footage with their *Pro/Con Package Homes* which spread across every available inch of standard suburban lots. Doug Jackson, on the other hand, has left the yard intact but capitalized on the space above. His *casa vertical* soars three stories above its tiny lot and is accessed by a hydraulic floor plate, minimizing the building's area.

Innovative solutions may also be found in the variety of flexible and mobile border dwellings which fit in anytime, anywhere. These include N55's *spaceframe*, a latticed structure which may be erected in virtually any location for the price of a small car, and Martín Ruiz de Azúa's *Basic House*, a simple fabric cube that requires only a gust of wind to inflate its four walls. Likewise, Greg Lynn FORM's *Embryologic House* ©™ is digitally designed to fit the most unusual of sites and openoffice & copehagenoffice's *NHEW PAD* needs no fixed foundation other than the box in which it is packed. with so many ways to stake a claim, life among the masses doesn't have to be an either/or scenario.

DOUG JACKSON, LARGE

casa vertical, Los Angeles, California, USA, 2000

TOP THE EXTERIOR OF *CASA VERTICAL* IS VERY NARROW, WHICH RESULTS IN A GENEROUS AMOUNT OF OUTDOOR SPACE— MORE THAN WOULD TYPICALLY SURROUND A HOUSE ON A LOT OF THIS SIZE.

OPPOSITE TOP THE HEIGHT OF *CASA VERTICAL* MAKES IT A PERFECT OBSERVATION TOWER FOR THE NEARBY AIRPORT RUNWAY.

OPPOSITE BOTTOM THE FLOOR PLATE CAN BE RAISED AND LOWERED HYDRAULICALLY TO MEET ANY OF THE DOMESTIC FACILITIES THAT ARE STOWED AWAY IN A SINGLE WALL OF THE HOUSE.

Unlike its neighbors, who shun their proximity to Los Angeles International airport, *casa vertical* embraces its location and was in fact conceived to make the most of the busy air traffic over the Westchester district of L.A. It therefore comes as little surprise that the client who commissioned Doug Jackson's proposal was a recently retired aeronautical engineer and flight enthusiast who wanted a grandstand view of the nearby runway.

The client's request for his home to be tall enough to provide a viewing platform of the airport, and the seemingly contradictory stipulation for the top floor to remain fully accessible as the client aged and became less able to climb stairs, shaped the extraordinary interior of *casa vertical*.

The house is designed around a hydraulic floor plate, which negates the need for stairs in the thirty-two-feet-high structure and, far more radically, dispenses with the notion of separate rooms. The interior of *casa vertical* is a single, generous space that adapts to suit any domestic activity. The essential facilities, including kitchen, shower, lavatory, laundry, and bed, are all stacked in the north wall of the house. The floor plate can be raised and lowered accordingly to meet each station depending on which activity the client wishes to undertake. This vertical arrangement of facilities minimizes the building's floor area and makes it an attractive proposition for other tight urban spaces. The reduced footprint of *casa vertical* means the rest of its plot can be retained as a usable outdoor space.

Jackson readily admits that the use of elevators and other lifting devices within a domestic setting is not a new phenomenon. Such machines are often inserted into homes for the elderly and disabled to aid mobility. However, the industrial aspect of this type of device is often disguised so as not to take away the homey quality of its location. Rarely is an industrial mechanism of such scale incorporated into the fundamental basis of a home as is proposed in *casa vertical*.

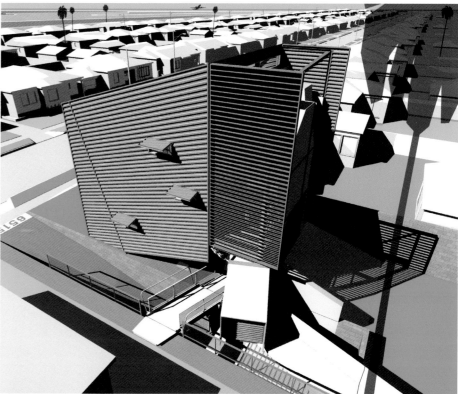

COELACANTH & ASSOCIATES

space Blocks kamishinjo, osaka, japan, 2001

space Blocks kamishinjo maximizes the potential of a tight, irregular plot of land in a densely populated suburb of osaka. The design provides a simple solution to the need for daylight and fresh air in a restricted space, while also ensuring the inhabitants' privacy. coelacanth developed an interactive design tool they call the "Basic space Block" to make the most of the kamishinjo site. The tool replaces drawn plans and sections with small cubes to communicate ideas between the client and the designer. The architects found that this three-dimensional approach effectively stimulates ideas concerning the relationship between a space and its usage. The blocks can be arranged in an infinite number of combinations to make the most of any given site, no matter how small or irregular. At kamishinjo, rather than allowing each different floor level to be confined to a flat plane, coelacanth have introduced cubic voids to extend beyond the floor plans and jut out of exterior walls in order to create extra living space.

The playful appearance of the *space Blocks kamishinjo* is a reflection of the hands-on approach taken in its conception. The unusual exterior protrusions—created by grafting on extra rooms in seemingly hovering capsules—echoes the clip-ons and slave units employed in the mobile structures of Atelier van Lieshout (p. 96). comparisons can also be drawn to the plug-in housing of kisho kurokawa's *Nagakin capsule Tower* built in Tokyo in 1972, but the modular approach to house design was established in Japan long before that. The traditional Japanese house, from the size and shape of internal areas to the dimensions of the house itself, was established around the module of the tatami, a rice-straw mat measuring seventy-one by thirty-five and a half inches. coelacanth have devised a complex modular approach to prefabricated dwellings that adds to an already impressive array of industrialized construction methods applied to housing in Japan.

kazuhiro kojima of coelacanth & Associates stated in 2000 that "Architecture is no longer being considered as a closed package but an interactive and delicate response to the city." The *Basic space Block system* achieves this by handing greater control of home design to the end user. The tool enables the client to visualize his or her final dwelling much more effectively and encourages the pushing of structural boundaries to maximize the available space.

MICHAEL RAKOWITZ

parasites, Boston, Massachusetts, 1998, and New York City, USA, 1999 & ongoing

RIGHT JOE H. UNPACKS HIS *parasite* SHELTER AND ATTACHES IT TO THE OUTTAKE DUCT OF A CITY BUILDING'S HVAC (HEATING, VENTILATION, AND AIR CONDITIONING) SYSTEM.

OPPOSITE THE WARM AIR LEAVING THE HVAC DUCT QUICKLY INFLATES JOE H'S *parasite* AND HE IS ABLE TO BED DOWN FOR THE NIGHT INSIDE HIS HEATED SHELTER.

Michael Rakowitz, lives and works in New York, USA

There is no segment of today's population more mobile than the homeless, who by choice, illness, or circumstance find themselves constantly on the move and in desperate need of housing—and who are discriminated against simply because they have none. Artist Michael Rakowitz has responded with temporary inflatable shelters, called *parasites*, which he distributes free of charge. Made of plastic bags and tape, on a budget of $5 per unit, the shelters are conspicuous visible protests against the condition of homelessness and help to prolong the lives of those affected by it.

In a manner similar to biological parasites, Rakowitz's shelters glom onto the HVAC outtake ducts of public buildings, "sucking" in otherwise unused urban air. Inspired by tents in Bedouin encampments, which are constructed in consideration of wind patterns, the shelters have double membranes, which harness the warm exhaust to inflate and heat their living spaces.

All of the shelters are custom-built, with height and shape being the direct result of private consultations with individuals. The first prototype, constructed in Cambridge, Massachusetts, out of black trash bags, was initially rejected by Bill S., a homeless man who did not want to sleep in a completely opaque shelter for fear of being attacked. As he pointed out, "homeless people do not have privacy issues, but rather security issues....we want to see and be seen."

In New York City, the structure was redesigned for Michael M., in direct response to then-Mayor Rudolph Giuliani's anti-homeless laws. Under Giuliani's mandate, any structure higher than three and a half feet was considered a tent and therefore an act of illegal camping. Michael M.'s shelter circumvented Giuliani's ordinance by being lower to the ground like a sleeping bag. Although he was ticketed twice for using the enclosure, in both instances the court threw out the charges, agreeing with his argument that the structure was a "body extension."

For Rakowitz, whose work is "shaped by [his] interaction as a citizen and artist with those who live on the street," only a complete redesign of social programs and municipal services combined with innovations in affordable housing would begin to solve the problem of homelessness. For the meantime, his visibly parasitic devices ensure that those affected will always be in the public eye. Being "seen" is half way to being equal.

TOP THE SHAPE OF THIS *parasite* RESEMBLES A SWOLLEN SLEEPING BAG, WHICH HAS PROVED CRUCIAL IN COURT IN DETERMINING WHETHER THE STRUCTURE IS AN EXTENSION OF THE BODY, LIKE AN ITEM OF CLOTHING, OR AN ILLEGALLY PARKED TENT.

BOTTOM AND OPPOSITE BILL S.'S IGLOO-LIKE SHELTER IS MUCH MORE VISIBLE THAN OTHER MODELS. HIS CONSPICUOUS HOME COMMUNICATES A REFUSAL TO SURRENDER AND REMINDS THE PASSERS-BY THAT HE'S STILL HERE.

michael rakowitz, lives and works in new york, usa

PIERCY CONNER ARCHITECTS

Microflat, London, England, 2002

TOP COMPUTER RENDERING OF A *MICROFLAT* COMMUNITY. THE STACKS OF FLATS MAY BE SLOTTED INTO ANY NUMBER OF EXISTING URBAN GAPS.

OPPOSITE TOP FOR WORKING PROFESSIONALS WITH NOT MUCH CASH TO SPARE, THE *MICROFLAT* IS A SMALL BUT STYLISH ALTERNATIVE TO LIVING IN THE 'BURBS.

OPPOSITE BOTTOM FLOOR PLAN OF THE STANDARD *MICROFLAT* UNIT ILLUSTRATING THE DIVISION OF LIVING SPACE.

Although industrialized countries have come a long way since the nineteenth century in improving the living conditions of their citizens, today's burgeoning inner cities are still as crowded and pricey as ever. London, in particular, tops the chart as Europe's most expensive, if not most densely populated, city in which to buy private housing—a fact which concerns Piercy Conner Architects. With property prices skyrocketing and mortgages harder to obtain, many key workers such as teachers and nurses are being driven to the margins (or further to the suburbs) and denied the cultural advantages of life in the big city where their services are desperately needed.

Piercy Conner have responded to this growing problem with their socially motivated *Microflat*, a dwelling that has sparked some criticism but which is intended to aid people in the lower salary ranges get a foothold in the property market. The *Microflat* offers young professionals the chance to stay in town by living in a "small, efficiently designed, high-quality, compact dwelling that is around two-thirds the size of a conventional inner-city, one-bedroom flat." Simply put, "micronauts" must make do with a 330-square-foot, oblong room divided into thirds: bedroom, kitchen/bath, and living/dining room. Groups of units are stacked on top of each other into self-sustaining complexes which can be slotted into previously uninhabitable spaces, such as the roofs of public buildings.

The controversial part involves who owns the flats. The rules of purchase are dictated and controlled by the architects, who have already barred anyone who already owns a home or makes more than £30,000 a year. This is a new twist on the traditional architect-client relationship, which situates Piercy Connor in the atypical role of social worker, real estate agent, and property manager. But according to the firm, their involvement will keep the prices down and profiteers out.

With the *Microflat*, the West will finally get a taste of the capsule cities the Japanese have been building since the 1960s, all of which are tiny modular units with well-designed interiors. The fact remains, too, that in action-packed cities from Tokyo to London, inhabitants do most of their "living" in offices, pubs, restaurants, and large parks. So perhaps all one needs is a clean, well-lighted place to catch the news and sleep.

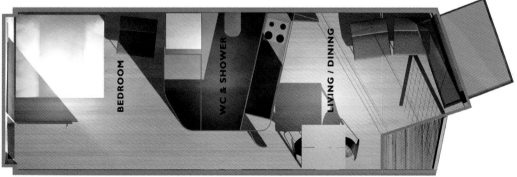

BEDROOM

WC & SHOWER

LIVING / DINING

STEFAN EBERSTADT

rucksack house, munich, germany, 2002

  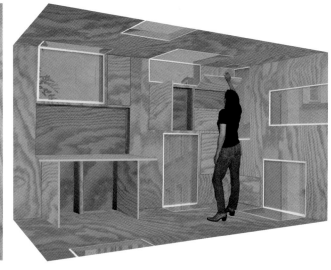

True to its name, *rucksack house* by German sculptor stefan eberstadt functions much like its nylon cousin, the backpack, clinging to its host with straps and providing concealed space for personal belongings. The mini house hangs in front of the windows of one-room apartments—the claustrophobic inner-city domain of students or temporary workers—and, through a host of flip-out furnishings and a multitude of openings, provides extra living space and direct access to daylight. Like a backpack, the house moves when its owner moves, next door or to another country.

Roughly eighty square feet in size, the suspended box is made from standard, four-by-eight-foot sheets of plywood, which are hinged to an aluminum frame and punctuated by plexiglas inserts. Inside, sections of the walls unfold, with the help of hidden magnets, into a desk, shelves, and a platform for reading or sleeping. The dwelling itself is lashed to the

chimney of its host with thick, reinforced nylon straps of the type used by construction workers to lift heavy crates. Looking like a cross between temporary scaffolding and a minimal sculpture, the *rucksack house* is perched between art and architecture, form and function.

Although the *rucksack house* is a fully functioning living space, its design is the result of a fundamental artistic question: How can sculpture function outside the context of art? Eberstadt's use of montage plays an integral role in the answer. Using a digital camera, he photographed buildings, pieces of plywood, metal framing devices, and even screws and hooks, which became the materials he used to build the home. After downloading the pictures on a computer, he used Adobe Photoshop to cut, paste, shape, and recombine imagery, textures, structures, and colors from the "real" world into a completely new form.

Although the "finished" home is virtual, it came into being exactly as his sculptures do, piece by piece and layer by layer on the computer. Like his British predecessors, the architecture collective Archigram, eberstadt uses montage to experiment freely with different materials and to try out a variety of real-world contexts in a playful manner before making any final decisions.

While his process differs somewhat from the expressionistic hands-on method of Robert Bruno (p. 26) or the found object approach of vito Acconci (p. 54), eberstadt's underlying question is the same: where does sculpture apply in today's world? With a prototype of *rucksack house* scheduled for release this year, eberstadt's live-in sculpture will soon provide a concrete answer to that question.

LOT/EK

Guzman Penthouse, Manhattan,
New York City, USA, 1996

Like many other practices described in this book, LOT/EK is establishing its credentials outside the customary architectural realm. Much of their work to date has appeared as art installations and interior renovations, but the *Guzman Penthouse* is a fully functioning, lived in, family home.

The house nestles on top of an existing loft apartment directly under the Empire State Building and enjoys an exceptional panorama of the surrounding cityscape. An arrangement of modified freight containers was added to the existing structure to create a master bedroom and an outdoor patio. The existing loft space now houses an open-plan living, dining, and kitchen area, as well as a separate child's bedroom. The added components are stacked above this space and effectively create another floor accessed via an internal fire escape ladder.

The *Guzman Penthouse* encompasses LOT/EK's passion for finding new applications for industrial containers that once served a different purpose in their former life. The use of retired objects in the *Guzman Penthouse* revitalizes the materials and enriches the texture of the home while also permeating it with a tremendous energetic force.

Although LOT/EK often operate in the context of installation art, their work, like Studio Orta (p. 112) and Atelier Van Lieshout (p. 96), is astonishingly practical and harbors, as Ada Tolla, the studio's co-founder states, "a level of commitment to reality." LOT/EK's salvaging of industrial leftovers for use in domestic contexts serves as a declaration to the dynamic punch attained by an ad-hoc approach to architecture. It is a spirited reminder to town planners everywhere that the urban landscape soon becomes sterile when a formal, utopian order is imposed upon it.

N55

spaceframe & Floating platform,
copenhagen, denmark, 1999 & ongoing

N55, copenhagen, denmark

ACCORDING to the members of the Rotterdam-based art collective N55, "concentrations of power" such as the government and the building industry have as much a bearing on the form and function of today's homes as architectural practice. The group refutes the commonly held notion that home ownership represents success, security, and stability. On the contrary, they suggest it represents the repression and control of individuals by greater powers whose interests are best served by a monopoly of standardized, high-priced housing.

In an effort to skirt the schemes of developers and keep the means of production firmly in the hands of the people, Ingvil Aarbakke, Jon Sørvin, Rikke Luther, and Cecilia Wendt have designed, constructed, and now inhabit the *spaceframe*—a portable, low-cost, maintenance-free house that can be built, dismantled, relocated, and enlarged numerous times by any layman—which costs as much as a small car.

True to its name, the *spaceframe* is a lattice-based structure whose strength and integrity depend not on gravity but on radical geometry, which is typically reserved for satellites and space platforms. N55 have brought this technology out into the open. Comprising two tetrahedra and one octahedron, which form the basic frame, their house is faced with plates of acid-resistant stainless steel and lined with moisture-absorbing fiberboard. When not in use, the house breaks down into neat stacks, which can be easily stored beneath a friend's sofa or in a box. This lends the home a flexibility and mobility not possible with conventional housing and allows it to fit in virtually anywhere: behind an existing home, in an alley, or on a rooftop. With the addition of a buoyant *Floating Platform*, the home may even be moored in a pond, lake, reservoir, or harbor. How big the home is, where it is located, and for how long are entirely up to its owner.

Like its commercial contemporaries, such as The Monolithic Dome Institute (p. 84), American Ingenuity (p. 44), and Earthship Biotecture (p. 70), N55 provides complete technical specifications and instructions for constructing the *spaceframe* and *Floating Platform* in manuals located on their web site. But because the group believes in sharing knowledge and know-how, they never charge for the information. They even refuse to patent their work, preferring instead to actively publicize it so that their "product" remains free and available to everyone. Unlike other homes on the market, the *spaceframe* is not for sale, so if you want to live in one, you must literally take the matter into your own hands.

MARTÍN RUIZ DE AZÚA

BASIC HOUSE, prototype dwelling, no fixed address, manufactured by PAÏ THIO, 1998

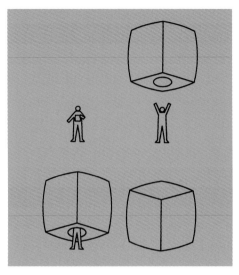

TOP RIGHT THE *BASIC HOUSE* CAN BE SCRUNCHED UP SMALL ENOUGH TO FIT IN YOUR POCKET. WHEN REQUIRED YOU JUST UNRAVEL IT, INFLATE IT, AND THROW IT ON LIKE A SWEATER.

BOTTOM RIGHT *BASIC HOUSE* HAS A REVERSIBLE COATING WITH GOLD ON ONE SIDE AND SILVER ON THE OTHER—GOLD TO INSULATE AGAINST THE COLD AND SILVER TO REFLECT THE HEAT.

OPPOSITE AZÚA IS INSPIRED BY CULTURES THAT MAINTAIN A MORE DIRECT RELATIONSHIP WITH THEIR ENVIRONMENT AND HAS PARED DOWN *BASIC HOUSE* TO INCLUDE ONLY THE ESSENTIAL ELEMENTS OF SHELTER.

If you have ever wondered exactly how difficult it is to fight your way out of a paper bag then a sparring session inside MARTÍN RUIZ DE AZÚA's *BASIC HOUSE* might give some indication. *BASIC HOUSE*, as the name suggests, strips the very fabric of the house to its most fundamental elements. It is simply a self-contained, cubic room that obviates the need for any structural components other than air.

Measuring only seventeen cubic feet when fully inflated, *BASIC HOUSE* will fit into the smallest of spaces. In order to erect the dwelling, one simply unravels the reversible polyester fabric from its pocket and decides which of the two finishes best suits the current climate. One side is finished in gold to insulate from the cold and the other silver to shield against heat. A slight breeze is all it takes to inflate the house and render it inhabitable.

During the daytime the house remains inflated by the action of body and solar heat, whereas at night it slowly deflates to form a protective blanket.

The swollen cube of metallic foil, with its myriad reflections in the crinkled surface, is simple and beautiful. The metallic fabric has a finish similar to that of the material used to protect satellites from the extreme conditions of space. Indeed, *BASIC HOUSE* has an extra-terrestrial presence due to its looming, floating form and it being in constant motion.

With *BASIC HOUSE*, MARTÍN RUIZ DE AZÚA urges us all to reconsider the amount of clutter we fill our homes with. He questions the need for so many cumbersome possessions and suggests instead "a life of transit without material ties. Having it all while hardly having anything."

MARTÍN RUIZ DE AZÚA, BARCELONA, SPAIN

JONES, PARTNERS: ARCHITECTURE

pro/con package homes, suburbia, california, usa, 2000 & ongoing

TOP THE CONNECTIVE TISSUE BETWEEN THE CONTAINERS REMAINS UNPROGRAMMED, USER-DEFINED SPACE.

BOTTOM DETAIL OF THE BACK SIDE OF THE "SHORT STACK" MODEL.

OPPOSITE THE "SHORT STACK" COMPRISES SEVEN CONTAINERS WHICH ARE MOUNTED ONTO THE RAIL SYSTEM ON WHICH THEY WERE DELIVERED. THE SPACE UNDERNEATH PROVIDES AMPLE ROOM FOR PARKING OR FUTURE ADDITIONS.

FOLLOWING PAGES "TOWER" MODEL AND "RANCH" MODEL.

one of the most prolific by-products of industry—the shipping container—is already in use around the globe as low-cost housing and relief shelter (see *global peace containers*, p. 52 and *future shack*, p. 100). soon it may be coming to a neighborhood near you. with a prototype scheduled for release this year, the new frontier of the american suburb may well be jones, partners: architecture's *pro/con package homes*.

with names like "ranch," "tower," and "short stack," the houses consist of up to fourteen standard shipping containers, with starter homes typically comprising six. the containers are purchased from used dealerships or brand name manufacturers, such as ikea or sears, and then assembled on site by a local contractor. they may be laid end to end or stacked seven high on the rail system which served as the means of their delivery. the resulting compound literally overtakes and exploits every available inch of the standard tract on which it is situated, exchanging front and backyards—which are nothing more than empty zones one crosses to get to a house—for

underground parking and space for additions.

the *pro/con* concept is predicated on a "loose fit" between the prefabricated containers and the manner in which they are configured. in contrast to *future shack* or *global peace containers*, which encourage end users to customize the containers themselves, *pro/con* homes allow buyers to specify how the connective tissue between their units will be programmed. owners can't control the manufacture of the modules, but they can have a say in how the modules are put together— something not possible in the current tract home market.

one of the more radical aspects of owning a *pro/con* home is that it exposes one's personal taste and buying habits to the rest of the neighborhood. in today's consumer world, where what you buy is who you are, there is no surer way of expressing your values than with "branded" containers. personalizing through product logos is nothing new, it's just never been so billboard blatant, commanding the visual space of the lot as much as the house dominates the physical area.

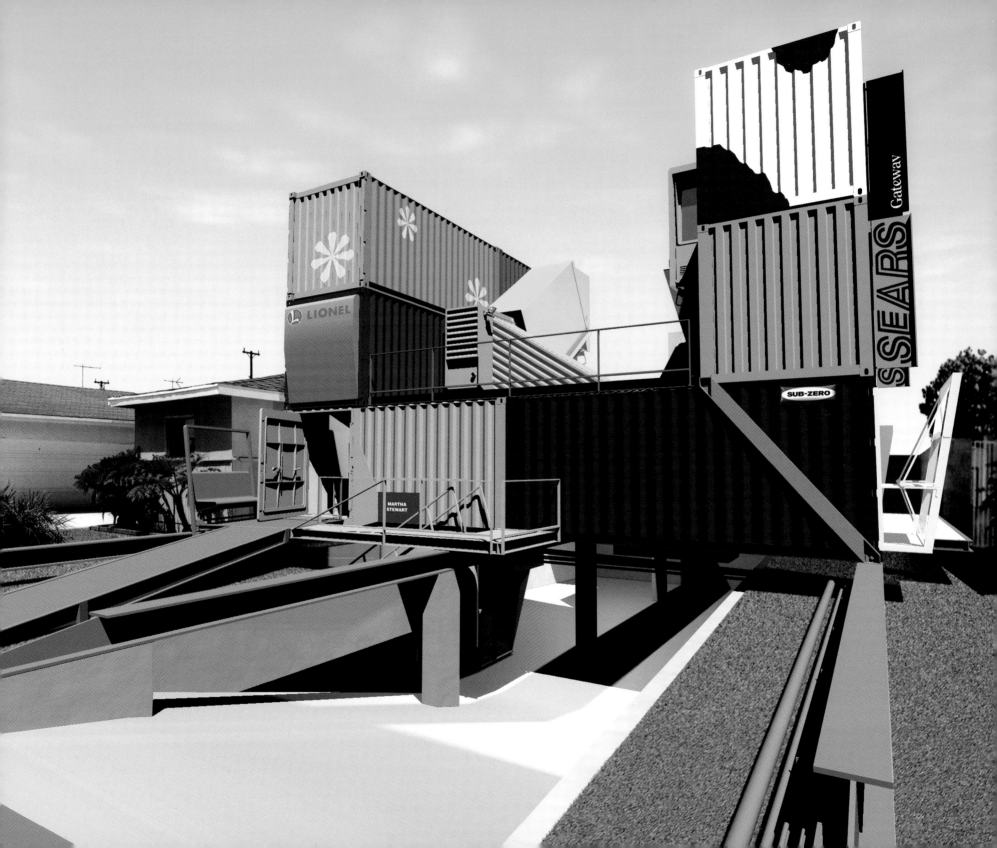

JONES, PARTNERS: ARCHITECTURE, EL SEGUNDO, CALIFORNIA, USA

OPENOFFICE & COPENHAGENOFFICE

nhew pad, 1999 & ongoing

TOP PHOTO DOCUMENTATION OF THE INSTALLATION OF *NHEW PAD* IN ISHOJ, DENMARK, IN JANUARY OF 2000. ALL OF THE MATERIALS REQUIRED TO ASSEMBLE THE UNIT MAY BE SHIPPED TO ANY LOCATION IN ONE BOX, WHICH LATER BECOMES PART OF THE HOME. THE MATERIALS THEMSELVES LEAD DOUBLE LIVES: THE STORAGE CRATE BECOMES A BED, BACKPACKS BECOME FURNITURE, AND PACKING MATERIAL IS USED FOR CUSHIONS AND INSULATION.

RIGHT THE COMPLETED, ONE-ROOM DWELLING MEASURES 10 X 6 X 12 FEET AND CAN BE AS DECADENT OR PRACTICAL AS ITS OWNER DESIRES.

when we think about home furnishings, rarely do we consider our homes themselves as pieces of instant furniture. that is precisely the concept behind *nhew pad*, a crate that contains all the materials and tools you need to erect a home within one day and is in itself part of the structure. a cross between self-assembly furniture and the pop-up tents and tables of campgrounds, *nhew (northouse eastwest) pad* is the ultimate all-in-one kit for laying down roots, however permanent, in virtually any setting.

the concept is novel: simply log on to the nhew design web site, select the materials that will comprise your home—options include felt, fleece, faux fur, foam, nylon, and aluminized polyethylene—then wait for the parts to be delivered (ready to go in one box) to any location you specify. this mix and match approach gives potential home owners the luxury of customization that is already a staple of the automobile and fashion industries. in fact, *nhew pad's* creators think of their unit as "architectural space tailored as an item of clothing."

once the made-to-order crate arrives, the contents are merely unpacked, unfolded, and/or snapped into place around the emptied shell, resulting in a fully functioning one-room dwelling, which simultaneously serves as a bedroom, living room, and kitchen. since the unit is compact and may be broken down, stored, and reassembled, it also serves as the perfect addition to an existing home, a temporary roof apartment, guesthouse, greenhouse, or weekend retreat.

what began as a research project in the extreme landscape of thule, greenland, where the nomadic inuit culture has thrived for more than a thousand years, is now making inroads into postindustrial countries obsessed with the contemporary products of nomadic lifestyle, from mobile phones to onboard navigational systems. in a strange turnabout, what would be considered substandard housing in impoverished nations is now being touted as smart housing in the west.

tanja jordan, linda taalman, and alan koch – openoffice, new york city, and copenhagenoffice, denmark

GREG LYNN FORM

Embryologic House© ™,
prototype dwelling, 1998

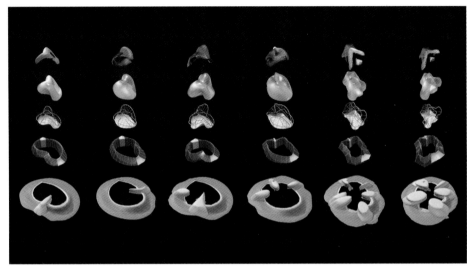

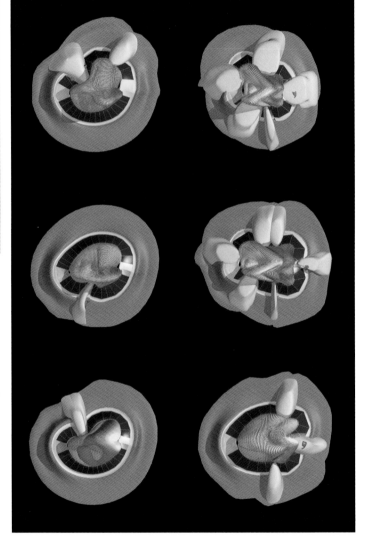

TOP THERE ARE ENDLESS POSSIBILITIES FOR THE LAYOUT OF EACH HOUSE. THE INDIVIDUALLY SHAPED INNER CHAMBERS ARE SHOWN HERE IN A VARIETY OF ARRANGEMENTS.

BOTTOM A MODEL SHOWING THE HOUSE SITED IN A LANDSCAPED GARDEN. THE COMPLEX, SHREDDED WINDOWS ARE MADE POSSIBLE BY ROBOTIC MILLING.

"Blobular" is probably the best term to describe the biomorphic shape of Greg Lynn FORM's *Embryologic House*. This digitally designed and manufactured dwelling is extremely flexible and can be sculpted to fit even the most unusual of sites.

Greg Lynn FORM used computer numerically controlled (CNC) machines to manufacture a prototype version of *Embryologic House* for the Venice Biennale of Architecture, 2000. This model was carved out of a solid block of foam using a robotic mill that allows for total precision and custom manufacture. The production process employed in this prototype marks a radical change in the way homes are commissioned, designed and built. Greg Lynn FORM pushes the boundaries of construction technology to demonstrate how homes can be prefabricated on a mass scale yet still retain a tailor-made individuality that means no two houses are the same.

The dynamic of the Greg Lynn FORM practice is structured around a collaborative approach drawing on pools of expertise from different disciplines. The studio believes this approach to be the most appropriate model for continued success in the future. This represents a prevailing attitude and is in accord with other contemporary practices, including FAT (p. 22), PO.D (p. 110) and AVL (p. 96).

The free-flowing form of the *Embryologic House* is a departure from the right-angled boxes most of us think of as home. The curvy dwelling with its system of shredded windows would have been prohibitively expensive to produce even as recent as a decade ago. This made-to-measure production process sweeps aside the notion that prefabrication equals homogeneity and has a real potential to revolutionize the whole construction industry.

GREG LYNN FORM, venice, california, USA

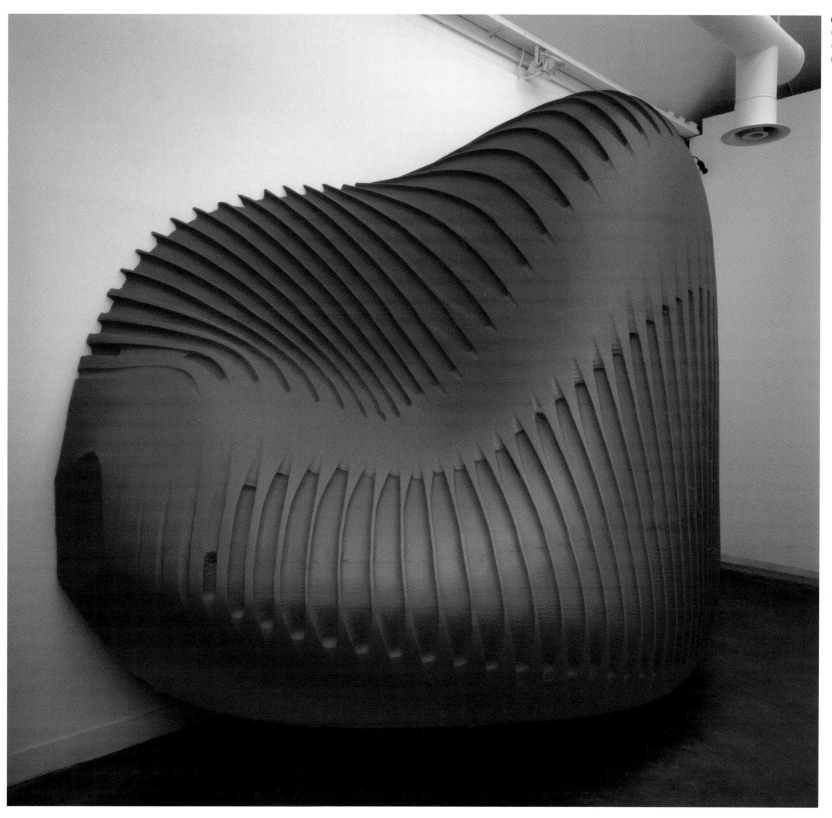

LEFT A CNC MILLING MACHINE WAS USED TO CARVE THIS 1/3 SCALE MODEL OUT OF A SOLID BLOCK OF FOAM.

USHIDA FINDLAY ARCHITECTS

Truss Wall House, Tsurukawa, Machida-city, Japan, 1991–93

TOP MAKING THE MOST OF A TINY PIECE OF LAND, USHIDA FINDLAY CONSTRUCTED A TWO-STORY HOME THAT RESEMBLES AN ORGANIC SCULPTURE.

OPPOSITE CURVING WALLS, AN OPEN STAIRWELL, AND A HOST OF BUILT-IN, CUSTOM FURNISHINGS GIVE THE IMPRESSION THAT THE HOME IS MUCH LARGER THAN IT ACTUALLY IS. THE STAIRS LEAD DOWN TO A BEDROOM AND, ON THE MAIN FLOOR, A LONG WALL LEADS TO A KITCHEN AND A ROUNDED SEATING AREA BENEATH A DOMED CEILING.

FOLLOWING PAGE GLASS DOORS OPEN ONTO AN INTIMATE COURTYARD WITH TILES MADE FROM COLORED MORTAR CAST IN BALLOONS.

one way of making space is to carve it out, a concept that informs the design of this house on a zero-lot-line property in suburban Japan. Like other commuter "bed towns" outside Tokyo, the suburb is a rather unattractive mash of mundane, detached family homes crammed onto tiny slices of land. However, by thinking sculpturally, Ushida Findlay Architects have transformed a small plot of land into a remarkably tactile and emotive environment which enables its occupants to tune out the visual and audible noise of the chaotic city and tune in to a tranquil private realm.

constructed for a young family, the home is a revolutionary departure from the cookie-cutter houses in the surrounding neighborhood whose facades face the busy streets. The house provides an enormous amount of seclusion by folding in on itself around a central courtyard. Like a sculpture, it twists and turns, providing an interior landscape of peace and serenity and enveloping and immunizing the residents from the sights and sounds of the nearby elevated commuter line. In many respects, the house looks as if it could have been thrown on a potter's wheel; however, it is the hand of computer-aided design (CAD) and cement-filled, wire mesh walls supported by trusses

Ushida Findlay Architects, Tokyo, Japan

that account for the home's precisely planned, free-flowing curves and abstract forms.

For all its openings and voids, the home contains a surprising amount of living space within its 1,100 square feet. Part of this is the result of super-efficient space planning and custom-designed furniture, such as a curved sofa which hugs the rounded wall in the living area and a cantilevered dining table. By far it is the optical arrangement of space that accounts for the feeling of openness in such tight quarters. Dynamic curves lead in and out, back and forth, from the ground-level bedrooms to the first-floor living area and kitchen, out into a private courtyard, and along a curving staircase up to a grassy roof garden. Simultaneously economic and sensuous, the *Truss Wall House* demonstrates that it is possible to achieve both individual identity and personal space within the modern anthill.

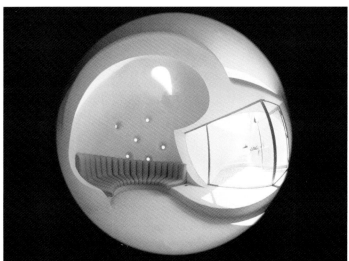

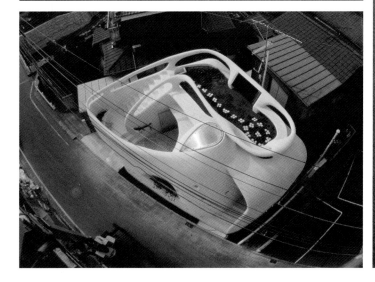

ushida findlay architects, tokyo, japan

BOTTOM ALTHOUGH USHIDA
FINDLAY'S *TRUSS WALL HOUSE*
EXTENDS TO THE VERY EDGES OF
ITS BUSY SITE, THE INTERIOR
SPACE IS ONE OF CALM AND
SERENITY.

BIBLIOGRAPHY

CHAPTER 1
SELF-CONSTRUCT

aga khan trust for culture "East wahdat upgrading programme, amman, jordan." aga khan development network, www.akdn.org, 1990.

bullivant lucy, pedro gadanho. *space invaders*. london: the british council, 2001.

cameron kristi. "living on the fringes." *metropolis magazine*, new york, august/september 2001.

davey peter. "the slick and the hairy." *architectural review*, london, january 2002.

kelly barbara m. *expanding the american dream: building and rebuilding levittown*. albany: suny, 1993.

leffingwell edward, karen marta. *modern dreams: the rise and fall of pop*. new york: the clocktower gallery, ps1, 1998.

lerner kevin. "sarah wigglesworth architects." *archrecord2*, www.archrecord.com, january 2002.

potrc marjetica. *east wahdat: upgrading program*, www.potrc.org, 1999.

salazar jamie, manuel gausa. *single family housing: the private domain*. barcelona: actar, 1999.

serageldin ismail, ed. *the architecture of empowerment: people, shelter, and liveable cities*. london: academy, 1997.

sudjic deyan. "the straw bale house." *domus*, issue 843, milan, december 2001.

till jeremy, sarah wigglesworth. *9/10 stock orchard street—a guide book*. london: the bank of ideas, 2001.

wolf karin, ed. *vito acconci: the city inside us*. vienna: mak, 1993.

CHAPTER 2
MOVE TO THE STICKS

"**archiprix international.**" *architectural review*, london, september 2001.

brizzi marco, "kas oosterhuis. il lato selvaggio dell'architettura." *arch'it*, www.architettura.supereva.it, italy.

"**case study house 10e**" *archrecord2*, www.archrecord.com, january 2002.

ibelings hans, ed. *die gebaute landschaft*. munich: prestel verlag, 2000.

migayrou, frédéric and marie-ange brayer, eds. *archilab: radical experiments in global architecture*. london: thames and hudson, 2001.

niesewand nonie. "architecture & imaging: softroom." *wallpaper magazine*, new york, september/october 1997.

nuttgens patrick. *the story of architecture*. london: phaidon, 1997.

parker freda. "life above the treetops at cloud hidden." www.monolithicdome.com/gallery/homes/kaslik.

richardson phyllis, lucas dietrich, ed. *xs: big ideas, small buildings*. new york: universe, 2001.

riley terence. *the un-private house*. new york: museum of modern art, 1999.

steiner dietmar. "lacaton & vassal." *domus*, issue 803, milan, april, 1998.

CHAPTER 3
BRING YOUR
OWN BUILDING

allen jennifer. "the new barbarians." *atelier van lieshout at camden arts centre*. london: camden arts centre, 2002.

allen jennifer. "vienna mealtime." *atelier van lieshout, schwarzes und graues wasser*. vienna: bawag foundation, 2001.

arieff allison. "we dream of prefabs...." *dwell*, san francisco, april 2001.

benjamin marina. "bags of potential." *the independent on sunday*, london, april 9, 2000.

cho hyoungjin, rémi feghali, and adrien raoul. "instant ego." www.geocities.com/instantego, 2000.

crosling john. "body architecture." *architectural review australia*, sydney, spring 1998.

ferreira anton. "sandbag homes may be shelter breakthrough." www.reuters.com, july 30, 2001.

ó hanluain daithí. "try living in the wheel world." *wired news*, www.wired.com, february 18, 2002.

heng whookiat, lotfi sidirahal. "nomambule." www.geocities.com/instantego/nomambule1, 2000.

lerner kevin. "the new nomadism." *archrecord2*, www.archrecord.com, october 2001.

van lieshout joep. Illustrated talk, camden arts centre, london, april 25, 2002.

luria rudolph, krzysztof wodiczko. "homeless conversations." homeless vehicle project, new york, 1988.

mestre marie-ève, stéphane magnin, christoph doswald, caroline maniaque, laurence flazon, and yves tenret. *air-air: celebrating inflatables*. monaco: le 27e stratagème, inflate unit research and grimaldi forum, 2001.

mills kindon. "holiday ramblings." *ten by ten*, volume 1 issue 2, chicago, fall/winter 2000.

orta lucy. "project summaries." http://studioorta.free.fr, 2002.

sanders mark. "lucy orta." *blueprint magazine*, london, may 1998.

santiago chiori. "house trailers." *smithsonian*, june 1998.

tommasini maria cristina. "corporal architecture, survival clothes." *domus*, issue 824, milan, march 2000.

trivedi bijal p. "dirt domes: breakthrough in emergency housing?" news.nationalgeographic.com, april 3, 2002.

virilio paul. "urban armour," *refuge wear*. paris: editions jean-michel place, 1996.

CHAPTER 4
SPACE INVADERS

eisaku ushida and kathryn findlay www.ellipsis.com/guides/tokyo/buildings/tokyo.truss.html

garreau joel. *edge city: life on the new frontier*. new york: doubleday, 1991.

guzmán pilar. "shelter." section f3, house & home, *the new york times*, february 14, 2002.

hawthorne christopher. "the lod/own on lot/ek." *metropolis magazine*, new york, august 2002.

jones wes. "towards a loose modularity." *praxis*, issue 3, cambridge, massachusetts, pp. 16–27.

lynn greg. *animate form*. new york: princeton, 1999.

scharrer eva. "michael rakowitz." www.mindspring.com, new york, 2001.

templeton david. "future shock." *north bay bohemian*, february 14–20, 2002.

welsh john. *modern house*. london: phaidon, 1995.

windsor antonia. "suite dreams." *time out*, london, april 17–24, 2002.

4x4: Apartment Avant-Garde. curated by kengo kuma, Dr. kisho kurokawa, and Dennis sharp, RIBA Architecture Gallery, London, England, october 9–November 28, 2001.

Air-Air. Grimaldi Forum, Monaco, July–September 2000.

Air en Forme. MU-DAC, Lausanne, switzerland, April–July 2000.

Atelier van Lieshout. camden Arts centre, London, England, April 26–June 16, 2002.

Hausschau, das Haus in der kunst (House show: The House in Art). curated by zdenek Felix, Deichtorhallen Hamburg, Hamburg, Germany, May 12–September 17, 2000.

Less Aesthetics, More Ethics. curated by massimiliano Fuksas, The 7th International Architecture Exhibition, venice, Italy, June 18–October 29, 2000.

Living in Motion. curated by mathias Schwartz-clauss, vitra Design Museum, weil am Rhein, Germany, Summer 2002.

science Fair. curated by sally o'Reilly, camden Arts centre, London, England, June 15, 2002.

space Invaders. curated by Lucy Bullivant and pedro Gadanho, The British council, exhibition tour opened at Galeria central Tejo–Museu de Electricidade, Lisbon, Portugal, september 2001.

The way we Live. RIBA Architecture Gallery, London, England, June 21–30, 2002.

The un-private House. curated by Terence Riley, museum of Modern Art, New York, USA, 1999.

Alles wird Gut: www.alleswirdgut.cc
American Ingenuity: www.aidomes.com
Martin Ruiz de Azúa: mrazua@teleline.es
Shigeru Ban Architects: www.dnp.co.jp
Briggs Port-A-Fold shelters Ltd.:
 www.cadvision.com
Dawson Brown Architecture:
 dba@carolinecasey.com.au
Robert Bruno: robertbruno10@yahoo.com
Cal-Earth: www.calearth.org
Coelacanth & Associates: www.c-and-a.co.jp
copenhagenoffice: www.copenhagenoffice.dk
Earthship Biotecture: www.earthship.org
stefan Eberstadt:
 stefan.eberstadt@adbk.mhn.de
FAT: www.fat.co.uk
Garofalo Architects: www.garofalo.a-node.net
Global Peace containers: www.gbs-gpc.com
Sean Godsell Architects:
 godsell@netspace.net.au
Architectuurstudio Herman Hertzberger:
 www.hertzberger.nl
Michael Hoenes: www.lesotho-tours.de
Doug Jackson, LARGE: la_rge@hotmail.com
Jones, partners: Architecture:
 www.jonespartners.com
Koeppel & Martinez:
 www.koeppelmartinez.com
Lacaton & vassal: lacaton.vassal@wanadoo.fr
Les Anthenea: www.waterventures.com
Atelier van Lieshout: www.avl-ville.com
LOT/EK: www.lot-ek.com
Greg Lynn FORM: www.glform.com
Monolithic Dome Institute:
 www.monolithicdome.com
N55: www.n55.dk
oosterhuis.nl: www.oosterhuis.nl,
 www.variomatic.nl
openoffice: www.open-office.net
studio orta: www.studio-orta.com
Valeska Peschke: valeskape@gmx.net
Piercy conner Architects:
 www.themicroflatcompany.com
PO.D: www.geocities.com/instantego
Marjetica Potrc: www.potrc.org
Michael Rakowitz:
 www.possibleutopia.com/mike
Rural studio:
 www.corrugatedconstruction.com
Jennifer siegal: www.designmobile.com
softroom: www.softroom.com
Ushida Findlay Architects:
 info@ushidafindlay.com
Sarah Wigglesworth Architects:
 www.swarch.co.uk
Krzysztof Wodiczko: wodiczko@mit.edu
Andrea Zittel: www.zittel.org

All reasonable efforts have been made to obtain copyright permission for the images in this book. If we have committed an oversight, we will be pleased to rectify it in a subsequent edition.

Frontispiece: softroom
p. 9: connie smith (top left), Jürgen Tesch (top right), stefan Eberstadt (bottom)
p. 10: stefan Eberstadt (top left), Archigram Archives (top right, bottom left)
p. 13: collection of stefan Eberstadt (top left), *st. Louis Post-Dispath* (top right), courtesy, The Estate of R. Buckminster Fuller (bottom left)
p. 15: courtesy, Ashley schafer, *Praxis* (top left), Nassau county Museum collection, Long Island studies Institute, Hempstead, New York (top right)
pp. 22–25: FAT
pp. 26–29: Robert Bruno
pp. 30–33: sarah wigglesworth
pp. 34–37: Doug Garofalo
pp. 38–39: michael Hoenes
pp. 40–41: courtesy Marjetica Potrc, ©matiya Pavlovec (left), ©jose Rodriguez (center)
pp. 42–43: koeppel & martinez
pp. 44–47: American Ingenuity
p. 48: Briggs Port-A-Fold Ltd.
p. 49: James winrow
pp. 50–51: openoffice
pp. 52–53: Richard J. L. martin
pp. 54–55: Barbara Gladstone Gallery
pp. 60–63: water ventures, california
pp. 64–67 courtesy shigeru Ban Architects, ©Hiroyuki Hirai
pp. 68–69 courtesy Robert Brown
pp. 70–71 courtesy epicscotland, ©Ashley coombes, ATOM (top left); Earthship Biotecture (all others)
pp. 72–75: softroom
pp. 76–77: Herman Hertzberger
pp. 78–79: kas oosterhuis
pp. 80–83: courtesy Lacaton & vassal, ©Philippe Ruault
p. 84: Jim kaslik (top left and right), Monolithic Dome Institute (all others)
p. 85: Jim kaslik
pp. 86–87: Monolithic Dome Institute
pp. 88–91: ©Timothy Hursley
pp. 96–99: courtesy Atelier van Lieshout, st beeldrecht
pp. 100–03: sean Godsell
pp. 104–07: valeska Peschke
pp. 108–09: Jennifer siegal
pp. 110–11: PO.D
pp. 112–15: studio orta

pp. 116–17: ©Gerwig Roth
pp. 118–19: courtesy Galerie Le Long
pp. 120–23: courtesy Andrea Rosen Gallery
pp. 124–27: Alles wird Gut
pp. 128–29: N55
pp. 134–35: Doug Jackson
pp. 136–39: courtesy coelacanth & Associates, ©satoshi Asakawa
pp. 140–43: michael Rakowitz
pp. 144–45: Piercy connor Architects
pp. 146–47: courtesy Rocket Gallery, London, ©stefan Eberstadt
pp. 148–49: courtesy LOT/EK, ©Paul warchol
pp. 150–51: N55
pp. 152–53: martín Ruiz de Azúa
pp. 154–57: wes Jones
pp. 158–59: courtesy openoffice, ©Andreas Pauly
pp. 160–61: Greg Lynn
pp. 162–65: All images courtesy Ushida Findlay Architects, ©katsuhida kida, ©shinkenchiku, and ©kenji kobayashi

THE AUTHORS AND PUBLISHER ARE VERY GRATEFUL TO THE FOLLOWING FOR THEIR HELP IN THE CREATION OF THIS BOOK:

VITO ACCONCI; THE AGA KHAN TRUST FOR CULTURE; ZURI AINZ; SAWAKO AKUNE, COELACANTH & ASSOCIATES; ALLES WIRD GUT; ALL THE FOLKS AT AMERICAN INGENUITY, INC.; ANDREA AND MARTA; SALLY ANN ARTHUR; MARTIN RUÍZ DE AZÚA; BRIGGS PORT-A-FOLD LTD.; ROBERT BRUNO; DAWSON BROWN ARCHITECTURE; CAL-EARTH; CARLYN, DANIEL, AND WENDY; CECILE AND TARA; SOPHIE CLINKARD, SOFTROOM; JOHN CONNELLY, ANDREA ROSEN GALLERY; RUI DIAS, CAS AALBERS, AND KAS OOSTERHUIS; STEFAN EBERSTADT; ELAN, AMBER, AND HER FAMILY; EMMA AND IVAR; SAM JACOB, FAT; REMI FÉGHALI, WHOOKIAT HENG, LOTFI SIDIRAHAL, ADRIEN RAOUL, AND HYOUNGJIN CHO, PO.D; ANNETTE FERRARA, *TENBYTEN*; PAT FISHER, TALBOT RICE GALLERY; HAYLEY FRANKLIN, SEAN GODSELL ARCHITECTS; HEATHER GALBRAITH, ISABELLE KING, AND LUCY WILSON, CAMDEN ARTS CENTRE; GAROFALO ARCHITECTS; GORDON, SARAH, JOSEPH, JOE, BEROL, AND IVY MARY; ANTOINE HAAG, WATER VENTURES; HERMAN HERTZBERGER; REBECCA HILL; MICHAEL HOENES; CURT HOLTZ, JAMES GIBBS, AND CHRIS WYNNE FOR BELIEVING IN THIS PROJECT; MARK HUGHES AND JENNIFER PARK, GALERIE LELONG; YUKIE IKEDA, SHIGERU BAN ARCHITECTS; DOUG JACKSON, LARGE; WES JONES, JONES, PARTNERS: ARCHITECTURE; JIM KASLIK; KAZUMI KOSEKO, USHIDA FINDLAY ARCHITECTS; KOEPPEL & MARTINEZ; KRISTIN AND JUSTIN; LACATON & VASSAL; PETRA LIGTENBERG AND CHARLOTTE MARTENS, ATELIER VAN LIESHOUT; BRUCE LINDSEY, AMY JO HOLTZ, AND HER FATHER FOR HELPING US FIND HER, RURAL STUDIO; GREG LYNN FORM; LYNNET, IAN, AND RHIANNON; MANDY, BILLY, GEMMA, POLLY, AND JAMES; ANNE MARTENS AND MARK CHALECKI; RICHARD MARTIN, GLOBAL PEACE CONTAINERS; LUCA MERCURI; D.J., MONOLITHIC DOME INSTITUTE; TOM MOODY, FOR BENDING AN EAR; CARTER MULL, BARBARA GLADSTONE GALLERY; MUM AND TONY; N55; NICOLA AND RICK; CHRIS NORRIS; LUCY ORTA AND ADELINE COUSIN, STUDIO ORTA; VALESKA PESCHKE; PETE AND MICHELLE; MARJETICA POTRC AND BARBARA PREDAN; SAM PRICE, PIERCY CONNER; MICHAEL RAKOWITZ; THE RANDALL FAMILY IN TEXAS AND LOUISIANA; MICHAEL REYNOLDS, KIRSTEN JACOBSEN, AND JONAH REYNOLDS, EARTHSHIP BIOTECTURE; SALLY RICKABY; NICOLA RONCONI; SID AND NATASHA; ASHLEY SCHAFER, HARVARD GRADUATE SCHOOL OF DESIGN; JENNIFER SIEGAL, OFFICE OF MOBILE DESIGN; LOUISE SLIMINGS; THE SMITH FAMILY, TEXAS; STUART SMITH AND JAMES WINROW, SMITH; JENNIFER STRATFORD; LINDA TAALMAN, OPENOFFICE; JEREMY TILL, SARAH WIGGLESWORTH ARCHITECTS; ADA TOLLA, LOT/EK; FELICITY WARBRICK; KRZYSZTOF WODICZKO AND ADAM WHITON; ANDREA ZITTEL; JAMES YOUNG, FOR TIRELESS PICTURE RESEARCH.